Top Careers in Two Years

Retail, Marketing, and Sales

Titles in the *Top Careers in Two Years* Series

Top Careers in Two Years

Retail, Marketing, and Sales

By Paul Stinson

Ferguson Publishing
An imprint of Infobase Publishing

Top Careers in Two Years
Retail, Marketing, and Sales

Ferguson
An imprint of Infobase Publishing
132 West 31st Street
New York, NY 10001

ISBN-13: 978-0-8160-6906-4
ISBN-10: 0-8160-6906-9

Library of Congress Cataloging-in-Publication Data

Top careers in two years.
  v. cm.
  Includes index.
  Contents: v. 1. Food, agriculture, and natural resources / by Scott Gillam — v. 2. Construction and trades / Deborah Porterfield — v. 3. Communications and the arts / Claire Wyckoff — v. 4. Business, finance, and government administration / Celia W. Seupal — v. 5. Education and social services / Jessica Cohn — v. 6. Health care, medicine, and science / Deborah Porterfield — v. 7. Hospitality, human services, and tourism / Rowan Riley — v. 8. Computers and information technology / Claire Wyckoff — v. 9. Public safety, law, and security / Lisa Cornelio, Gail Eisenberg — v. 10. Manufacturing and transportation — v. 11. Retail, marketing, and sales / Paul Stinson.
  ISBN-13: 978-0-8160-6896-8 (v. 1 : hc : alk. paper)
  ISBN-10: 0-8160-6896-8 (v. 1 : hc : alk. paper)
  ISBN-13: 978-0-8160-6897-5 (v. 2 : hc : alk. paper)
  ISBN-10: 0-8160-6897-6 (v. 2 : hc : alk. paper)
  ISBN-13: 978-0-8160-6898-2 (v. 3 : hc : alk. paper)
  ISBN-10: 0-8160-6898-4 (v. 3 : hc : alk. paper)
  ISBN-13: 978-0-8160-6899-9 (v. 4 : hc : alk. paper)
  ISBN-10: 0-8160-6899-2 (v. 4 : hc : alk. paper)
  ISBN-13: 978-0-8160-6900-2 (v. 5 : hc : alk. paper)
  ISBN-10: 0-8160-6900-X (v. 5 : hc : alk. paper)
  ISBN-13: 978-0-8160-6901-9 (v. 6 : hc : alk. paper)
  ISBN-10: 0-8160-6901-8 (v. 6 : hc : alk. paper)
  ISBN-13: 978-0-8160-6902-6 (v. 7 : hc : alk. paper)
  ISBN-10: 0-8160-6902-6 (v. 7 : hc : alk. paper)
  ISBN-13: 978-0-8160-6903-3 (v. 8 : hc : alk. paper)
  ISBN-10: 0-8160-6903-4 (v. 8 : hc : alk. paper)
  ISBN-13: 978-0-8160-6904-0 (v. 9 : hc : alk. paper)
  ISBN-10: 0-8160-6904-2 (v. 9 : hc : alk. paper)
  ISBN-13: 978-0-8160-6905-7 (v. 10 : hc : alk. paper)
  ISBN-10: 0-8160-6905-0 (v. 10 : hc : alk. paper)
  ISBN-13: 978-0-8160-6906-4 (v. 11 : hc : alk. paper)
  ISBN-10: 0-8160-6906-9 (v. 11 : hc : alk. paper)
  1. Vocational guidance—United States. 2. Occupations—United States. 3. Professions—United States.
  HF5382.5.U5T677 2007
  331.7020973—dc22

2006028638

Produced by Print Matters, Inc.
Text design by A Good Thing, Inc.
Cover design by Salvatore Luongo

Printed in the United States of America

Sheridan PMI 10 9 8 7 6 5 4 3 2 1

This book is printed on acid-free paper.

Contents

How to Use This Book

This book, part of the *Top Careers in Two Years* series, highlights in-demand careers for readers considering a two-year degree program—either straight out of high school or after working a job that does not require advanced education. The focus throughout is on the fastest-growing jobs with the best potential for advancement in the field. Readers learn about future prospects while discovering jobs they may never have heard of.

An associate's degree can be a powerful tool in launching a career. This book tells you how to use it to your advantage, explore job opportunities, and find local degree programs that meet your needs.

Each chapter provides the essential information needed to find not just a job but a career that fits your particular skills and interests. All chapters include the following features:

- "Vital Statistics" provides crucial information at a glance, such as salary range, employment prospects, education or training needed, and work environment.

- Discussion of salary and wages notes hourly versus salaried situations as well as potential benefits. Salary ranges take into account regional differences across the United States.

- "Keys to Success" is a checklist of personal skills and interests needed to thrive in the career.

- "A Typical Day at Work" describes what to expect at a typical day on the job.

- "Two-Year Training" lays out the value of an associate's degree for that career and what you can expect to learn.

- "What to Look For in a School" provides questions to ask and factors to keep in mind when selecting a two-year program.

- "The Future" discusses prospects for the career going forward.

- "Interview with a Professional" presents firsthand information from someone working in the field.

☞ "Job Seeking Tips" offers suggestions on how to meet and work with people in the field, including how to get an internship or apprenticeship.

☞ "Career Connections" lists Web addresses of trade organizations providing more information about the career.

☞ "Associate's Degree Programs" provides a sampling of some of the better-known two-year schools.

☞ "Financial Aid" provides career-specific resources for financial aid.

☞ "Related Careers" lists similar related careers to consider.

In addition to a handy comprehensive index, the back of the book features two appendices providing invaluable information on job hunting and financial aid. Appendix A, Tools for Career Success, provides general tips on interviewing either for a job or two-year program, constructing a strong résumé, and gathering professional references. Appendix B, Financial Aid, introduces the process of applying for aid and includes information about potential sources of aid, who qualifies, how to prepare an application, and much more.

Introduction

When you first think of jobs in retail, sales, and marketing, you might picture SpongeBob Squarepants flipping Crabby patties or Steve Carrell selling electronics at the mall in *The 40-Year-Old Virgin*. While the less-than-glamorous frontline jobs of cashier and stock boy may first jump to mind, this industry provides many more challenging occupations in a variety of settings. Working an entry-level position can give you some idea of the industry, but those who pursue a two-year education can advance to managerial positions and get on a rewarding career track.

Selling Never Sleeps

Opportunities abound for talented people pursuing employment in this area because those who can sell help boost profits—and that's just what corporate America wants! In fact, according to the U.S. Bureau of Labor Statistics (BLS), the number of jobs available in most of the fields we cover are expected to increase between 10 and 20 percent between now and 2014. Employment opportunities are projected to rise by

✔ 2.2 million jobs in management, business, and finance
✔ 1.4 million jobs in sales
✔ 1.1 million jobs in transportation and material moving

What's more, "retail" was listed as the category with the largest projected job growth between 2004–2014, increasing by 736,000 jobs or 17 percent over a 10-year period!

Credit the insatiable appetite of the business world and its need to expand and reach new markets for much of the expected boom in retail. Many entry-level jobs in these fields experience seasonal turnover, and those who learn their industry from the ground up can rise through the ranks of an organization. While a two-year degree can help get a foot in the door, major retailers often have their own management training programs that guide dedicated workers up the ladder.

What It Takes to Make It

For many, work in this area provides a stage for sharpening their entrepreneurial and social talents while learning how to work as a team player and master knowledge specific to their profession. Perhaps more than any other talent, communication is the most vital in this field. These professionals depend on speaking and writing skills to persuade and motivate employees and customers. Public relations specialists churn out press releases touting the benefits of their products; insurance agents explain why families need life insurance to financially protect their loved ones; sales managers may tell shoppers why a certain stereo, car, or sofa is perfect for their needs.

Those who excel in these jobs are not only strong communicators, they believe that what they're selling will genuinely help the customer. Whether they're real estate agents scurrying around in their car to meet home shoppers or advertising managers helping clients reach their audience, they take pride that their goods and services can make a positive difference in a person's life.

In addition, professionals in retail, sales, and marketing simply get a thrill from making a sale. They have some understanding of psychology and what makes a person make a purchase. Although you won't see the job of fortuneteller outlined in this book, every single one of the careers examined requires an element of forecasting. Those who can predict consumer trends and habits often gain an edge when it comes to boosting the bottom line. To hone this talent, workers devote time to studying market trends and becoming experts in their industry.

Another trait common to most of these fields is teamwork. From sales managers to marketing heads, these professionals rely on motivated coworkers to help execute plans. In addition to those they may supervise, many in this field work in tandem with managers on their own level, ensuring that plans align with the overall mission of the company. A public relations specialist, for example, typically needs to collaborate with marketers, advertisers, and management before unleashing a new media campaign.

Depending on the job, your day could follow a very traditional 9-to-5 work schedule, such as that of most marketing or advertising sales agents. On the other hand, real estate agents or e-commerce specialists keep hours that can resemble a doctor's schedule. Because these workers often are on call, from time to time they drop everything to rush across town to meet with a potential buyer or get a crashed computer system back up and running.

As far as work conditions are concerned, most operate in comfortable office settings. However, sales takes travel as well. Many of the careers profiled here demand a balance of time spent in the office with time spent on the road—perhaps working out of a hotel room before meeting with a client or attending an industry-related convention. Real estate and insurance agents especially put in the miles to meet with their customers.

If you're willing to invest the time at the entry level before getting the keys to the executive washroom or advancing to the back office, many fields (especially retail) reward those with patience and an appetite for learning.

You'd be surprised how often upper-level management mutters the old cliché about "good help being so hard to find these days." In some fields, employee turnover can be quite high and there is plenty of advancement opportunity for those who stick around and learn their industry. The HELP WANTED signs may not always be out or posted online, but good companies continuously keep an eye open for new talent. So, if you know someplace where you would like to work, by all means tune up your résumé, contact that firm's human resources department, and introduce yourself.

Get Web-Wise

Advances brought about by the Internet age have created new positions in retail, sales, and marketing. The Internet has unleashed a whole host of ways to provide goods and services and connect with niche markets. It usually only takes a few seconds of Web surfing to spot ads touting goods and services for sale online. Colleges and universities, life insurance, home mortgages, toys, CDs—you name it, you can shop for it via computer. (It's worth taking a look at some of the powerhouse Web "e-tailers" such as Amazon.com and Overstock.com who have mastered the art of the online sale.)

Even if your field isn't specifically that of an e-commerce professional, those who ignore the marketing and sales opportunities that the Internet provides run the risk of falling behind the competition. The Internet allows self-starting individuals opportunities to market and sell themselves (and their product) in ways never dreamed of 20 years ago. For example, a real estate agent or broker may have once depended solely on word-of-mouth or a smiling picture on a bus stop bench to support her business; but by developing a neighborhood-specific Web site supported by virtual tours, she has suddenly expanded her reach dramatically. Although an e-commerce specialist may need to master the computer coding of JAVA and C++, many skills needed to maintain a Web site are not that complicated.

Often the reputation of a business or individual largely depends on creating a community presence or awareness. A Web site can be part of this, and, as you read this book, you'll learn of many other marketing techniques. As Andy Warhol communicated in his portraits of repeated iconic figures (such as Campbell's soup, Elvis Presley, or Marilyn Monroe), the familiar can be fascinating, and familiarizing your client or customer with you or your brand is vital to establishing and retaining your clientele.

Put In the Time to Reap the Rewards

As is the case with many of the fields illustrated between these pages, being a self-starter is indispensable. If you don't make that extra effort to connect with a client or customer, someone else will. Our spotlighted public relations professional, Lara Stache, raised her value with her company by offering to start up a public relations department, which her employer did not have. Her company's presence in local, national, and industry media has been on the rise ever since.

We include only a sampling of retail, marketing, and sales careers in this volume. Others you might want to explore include copywriter, property manager, brand manager, purchasing agent, and claims adjuster.

Even though the job descriptions for these different business careers vary, common threads run through each: communication skills, determination, an interest in helping people, and personality. Whether you're a distribution professional consulting with your team at the warehouse or an insurance agent consulting with a family, you need to be a good listener and able to put yourself in either the shoes of your coworkers or of the clients and customers you're seeking to help.

Benefits of an Associate's Degree

When people think about the professions in sales, marketing, and retail, many mistakenly assume that most jobs require a four-year business degree. While it's certainly true that some professionals in these fields have advanced degrees, an associate's degree at an accredited community college, trade school, or technical school coupled with an internship or real-world work experience will give you the background needed to enter these fields.

In fact, the National Association of Colleges and Employers says that companies often prefer associate's degree graduates for several reasons. Graduates with two-year degrees often possess useful technical skill sets and typically need less training than other new graduates. They are more likely to enter the workforce with "hands-on" experience. Employers noted that associate degree graduates tend to have more work and/or "life" experience than traditional collegians. Some employers say that as a result of having experience, two-year grads tend to have developed a good work ethic—a quality that is often lacking in those with less experience.

The fact of the matter is that employers like to hire known quantities with good references and a track record of reliability and productivity. You can develop a track record, creative portfolio, or other body of work through internships or summer jobs related to your field. Part-time work and internships are great opportunities to road-test what you've learned in the classroom, show what you're capable of, and plug into a network of contacts and references who can connect you to a first job out of college.

Not only do these associate degree programs cost less money and require a smaller time commitment than traditional four-year schools, but such programs also offer a tailor-made curriculum designed to help students gain the skills they need to work in rewarding careers.

The time and effort needed to earn an associate's degree can produce tangible rewards: Students who earn an associate's degree tend to make

$2,000 to $6,000 a year more than those who try to get by with just a high school diploma.

For many students, the lower costs of community colleges play a key role in their decision on where to go. The average annual tuition and fees for attending a four-year public school in a student's home state was about $5,130 during the 2004–2005 school year while the tuition to attend a community college was about $2,080, according to a survey by the College Board. Students who attend schools away from home must also pay room and board fees, which at state schools ups the average tally to about $11,350 a year.

In addition, students who were not "A" students in high school often find a second chance to prove themselves at a two-year school. Admission requirements—GPA, SAT/ACT scores, etc.—are typically less stringent than at four-year institutions. Plus, such schools frequently provide special classes and tutors who can help students strengthen their basic academic skills in writing and math. Because the class sizes at community schools are typically smaller than those at universities, students often receive more personalized instruction.

Two-year schools also provide flexible scheduling, which can make it easier for some students to attend. Students who work during the day, for example, can often take classes at night. Those who attend a school nearby can save money by living at home, and at some schools, students can even take courses online.

At a community college, you can enroll in a program leading to an associate in arts or science (A.A. or A.S.) or an associate in applied science (A.A.S.) degree. To earn an A.A.S., you usually take specialized courses in fields such as construction technology, medical assisting, or electronics, as well as general education courses in subjects such as English and math.

During your two years of study, you'll take a mix of general college classes and career-based courses that will train you to work in your chosen career, whether as a market research analyst, fashion designer, or e-commerce specialist.

Some retail and sales programs offer a network of opportunities to work as interns or trainees during the summer or part time while attending school. Some careers offer certification classes in fields such as e-commerce and distribution, while real estate and insurance curriculums are geared toward helping students pass their state licensing test. Although you will be in the classroom for two years, some of these occupations require continuing education. For example, real estate and insurance agents often must take classes to stay current, while e-commerce specialists always have to keep up with new software or hardware tools of their trade.

If you have your heart set on working in this field, but don't want to pursue a two-year degree, some college programs award certificates to students who complete courses directly related to their chosen profession. For example, you can take crash courses in computer skills or in how to sell advertising. Other options include enrolling in state-required classes that act as preparatory courses for passing state licensing exams in real estate or insurance. These programs typically take six months to a year to complete.

Is a Career in Retail, Sales, or Marketing Right for You?

Ask yourself the following questions to see if the careers in this book might be right for you.

✔ Do you enjoy helping others?

✔ Can you handle pressure?

✔ Are you a problem solver?

✔ Are you a team player who can take direction from others?

✔ Are you a conscientious worker?

✔ Are you good with details?

✔ Do you have solid math skills?

✔ Can you anticipate trends?

✔ Are you organized?

✔ Can you plan things out several weeks in advance?

✔ Are you dependable (you've missed very few days of school or work)?

✔ Can you get along with different personalities?

✔ Do you like variety in your work?

✔ Do you enjoy business?

✔ Are you interested in how a company works?

✔ Are you a quick thinker?

✔ Are you flexible about your work schedules? (Would you be willing to work weekends or nights?)

If you answered yes to most of these, then a career in retail, marketing, or sales might be a perfect match.

Finding the Right School

A good place to start your search for a two-year college that fits your needs is online at http://www.collegeboard.com. You can key in specific criteria, such as the program you want to study or the area where you want to live, and it'll display options that meet your needs. You also can find information about colleges at libraries, which usually have college directories and individual catalogues. When you find a college that piques your interest, check out its Web site, look over its catalogue, and talk to someone at the school. If the school is nearby, you may even want to visit its campus to get a feel for the place.

Look for a school that is accredited by professional associations in your field. Unfortunately, some so-called diploma mills run fraudulent programs: They hand out worthless diplomas and certificates without teaching students the skills that they need to work in their chosen professions. To learn more about such fraudulent schools, check "Diploma Mills and Accreditation" at the U.S. Department of Education's Web site: http://www.ed.gov/students/prep/college/diplomamills/index.html. The Council for Higher Education Accreditation also offers helpful information at http://www.chea.org.

The best way to avoid such pitfalls is to enroll in accredited schools and programs. The following are top accrediting agencies for schools:

Accrediting Council for Independent Colleges and Schools, http://www.acics.org

Distance Education and Training Council, http://www.detc.org

Middle States Association of Colleges and Schools, http://www.msache.org/

New England Association of Schools and Colleges, http://www.neasc.org/

North Central Association of Colleges and Schools, http://www.ncahigherlearningcommission.org/

Northwest Association of Schools and Colleges, http://www.opi.state.mt.us/nascu/text.htm

Southern Association of Colleges and Schools, http://www.sacs.org

Western Association of Schools and Colleges, http://www.wascweb.org/

Plus, many business organizations offer accreditation and certification for specific retail, marketing, and sales programs. They include:
Accrediting Commission of the National Association of Trade and Technical Schools, http://www.accsct.org

Universal Accreditation Board (for Public Relations), http://www.praccreditation.org

Destination Marketing Association International, http://www.destinationmarketing.org

Asia-Pacific Risk and Insurance Association, http://www.apria.org

Allied Business School, Trade Schools, Colleges & Universities, http://www.trade-schools.net/allied-business-schools/accreditation.asp

International Advertising Association, http://www.iaaglobal.org

If you think there's a chance you might want to continue your schooling, make sure that most of the credits earned in the two-year program can be transferred to a four-year school. Someone with training in advertising, for example, can continue his training to become a creative director with more responsibility and a higher paycheck. Likewise, an insurance agent may decide to go back to school to become a financial analyst, which generally requires four years of school.

Retail, Sales, and Marketing Contacts

For general information on retail, sales and marketing, contact:

National Retail Federation, 325 7th Street NW, Suite 1100, Washington, DC 20004   http://www.nrf.com/retailcareers

American Purchasing Society, North Island Center, Suite 203, 8 East Galena Boulevard, Aurora, IL 60506   http://www.american -purchasing.com

American Association of Advertising Agencies, 405 Lexington Avenue, New York, NY 10174-1801   http://www.aaaa.org

Public Relations Society of America, 33 Maiden Lane, New York, NY 10038-5150   http://www.prsa.org

Retail, Wholesale, and Department Store Union, 30 East 29th Street, 4th Floor, New York, NY 10016   http://www.rwdsu.info.len

Retail Sales Manager

Vital Statistics

Salary: The median annual salary for retail sales managers is $32,720, according to 2006 data from the U.S. Bureau of Labor Statistics. Seasoned managers may earn more than twice that amount.

Employment: The number of jobs for supervisory sales workers is expected to grow at a slower pace than the average for all careers through 2014. Technology skills are essential in this computer-dependent marketplace.

Education: An associate's degree in retail management can be completed in as little as 12 months. Training includes the principles of accounting, marketing, communications, sociology, management, and sales. Some previous computer literacy would be helpful.

Work Environment: Many retail sales managers have offices within the stores, usually close to the areas they oversee. Atmospheres vary from plush and quiet high-end fashion boutiques and jewelry stores to crowded and noisy grocery stores and retail outlets.

Managing in the field of retail isn't just another day at the mall, corner store, or at-home business. It's about daily decision making, team building, and sharing your creative vision for brand innovation and growth. According to the 2005 U.S. Census Bureau survey, retail is the second-largest industry in the United States in terms of establishments and number of employees (excluding food and drink services), generating $3.719 trillion in annual retail sales. With so much at stake in an industry challenged by staff turnover, opportunities and advancement await those dedicated individuals who stay in the industry and become experts in their field and master the art of developing an effective team.

One of a sales manager's main duties is handling staff. They do the firing, hiring, scheduling, and sometimes the training of retail salespersons, cashiers, customer service representatives, and stock clerks. Managers assign duties to their staff and make sure they are doing their work correctly and on time.

Retails operations rise or fall on customer satisfaction, and managers are first in the line of duty to see that the customers are happy. They usually field all customer complaints, requests, and recommendations. They need to be amateur psychologists and sociologists as well, evaluating the customer's experience and anticipating future consumer trends so they can provide the best services and products and generate more profits. Managers may also take care of purchasing, budgeting, and accounting.

Salaries for retail sales managers typically start in the $30,000 range with a generous benefits package that includes medical, dental, and vision insurance and 401k savings plans. Department managers who have developed a track record of communicating the national marketing strategies while consistently meeting or beating sales targets can become candidates for middle and upper management. Although salaries vary by region and niche industry, district retail sales managers can earn a median salary of $70,000 per year; regional retail sales managers can pull in $110,000 per year; and "zone" retail sales managers at the top of the pyramid can typically earn $164,000 per year (Salary Wizard). Some who work in the field for a long time advance to become senior managers, and a few even wind up as store owners.

On the Job

A retail sales manager's job really depends on the type of product he or she is selling, and items can range from photographic equipment to alternative CDs to clothing for the Gap or Banana Republic. Because you're in charge of selling that product, hopefully it's something in which you're interested. Your enthusiasm and expertise in a product can help you increase sales. You also have to order items, check inventory, set up sales displays, and review monthly sales figures.

Success depends on your people skills as well. You have to motivate your staff each day to give their best, and you check their work to make sure their assigned duties are completed. Are clothes all ticketed with their sale prices? Is the promotion for the new Green Day album properly displayed? Are your cashiers at their posts? In addition to your employees, you're interested in keeping your customers happy. You're on the sales floor asking if they need any help, directing them to the aisle they need, and demonstrating products they're interested in buying—such as a TV or outdoor grill.

If you're at a big department store, you might have to meet with other managers and coordinate plans for your department with them. You may also report to a sales supervisor about the latest sales figures, promotional plans, staffing issues, and project profits for the next month.

Keys to Success

To be a successful retail sales manager, you should have:

- stellar communication skills (bilingual skills can help—especially Spanish)
- a passion for your brand

❧ the ability to motivate others

❧ strong organizational and business skills

❧ a willingness to work evenings, weekends, and odd hours as needed

❧ confidence and decisiveness

Do You Have What It Takes?

Students who are interested in starting a career in retail sales management love working with other people. If you're already a group leader and are talented at motivating others, this career could be a good match. You cannot mind being on your feet for long stretches and must have communication skills. You must find it easy to give instructions and explain things to others. A fondness for people-watching helps because part of your job is to identify customer trends and needs and observe employee performance. You should have an inclination to study communications, marketing, business, economics, and accounting.

A Typical Day at Work

Although your workday will vary with the type of goods or services you supply, a typical day for a retail sales manager might start by taking out your key and opening the store. Then, with a notepad in hand for jotting down thoughts, you walk through the store to assess the stock on the shelves, the sales displays, and overall condition of your store. You greet your employees as they come in and discuss any chores that need to be completed. Before you open to the public, you make sure that cashiers, floor sales people, and stock clerks are ready. As shoppers mill about, you answer questions, take care of a return, and demonstrate your biggest widescreen TV to a football fan and potential buyer. You take a half-hour off the sales floor in the afternoon to update information on the store's Web page. When closing time rolls around, you go over sales for the day with the cashiers and supervise general clean up.

How to Break In

Experience in retail sales is certainly important, and luckily it's easy to get because many stores seek to hire sales staff. You might even get a part-time job around the holidays, when retailers need to take on more help. Internships can go a long way toward connecting you to management opportunities. They provide management training, as well as a chance to build professional relationships and prove yourself as a worker. Two-year and even one-year schools emphasize the value of experience outside the classroom and can often connect you to an internship that suits your interests.

Two-Year Training

Many community colleges and private two-year schools offer associate's degree programs that will prepare students to become retail sales managers and merchandise marketers. Coursework emphasizes basic management principles and practices. Recommended courses include accounting, marketing, management, and sales, as well as psychology, sociology, and communication. Computer smarts are a must because almost all cash registers, inventory control systems, and sales quotes and contracts are computerized. Courses that zero in on manager skills will cover interviewing, customer service, employee and inventory management, and scheduling. Classroom exercises may focus on strengthening leadership and team-building abilities.

Many two-year schools supplement classroom work with concrete business experience. Time spent training in an actual store will not only add to your résumé but also offer a chance for building relationships that could lead to future employment. Note too that many bigger retailers have in-house management training programs, from which you may be able to benefit.

With an associate's degree, a graduate can work in the retail field as a buyer, regional manager, account coordinator, merchandise planner, planning analyst, assistant buyer, sales representative, assistant manager, showroom manager, operations manager, department manager, purchasing agent, or in advertising, marketing, promotions, and public relations.

What to Look For in a School

When considering a two-year school, be sure to ask these questions:

☞ What areas of specialization does the school offer for a career in retail (e.g., fashion apparel, fashion marketing, food service management, or retail management technology)?

☞ How relevant are the credentials of the school's faculty? Are they plugged into the type of retailing you want to join?

☞ What is the school's job placement rate, and where have graduates gone on to work?

☞ Are you in a location conducive to retail experiences that will build on your classroom instruction and add to your understanding of business?

The Future

Employment opportunities in the retail field are almost a constant because of the high amount of staff turnover as workers transfer to other positions and occupations. Expanding businesses and the motivation to drive sales with enhanced customer service will also create many new positions. According to the Bureau of Labor Statistics, the largest employers are grocery stores, department stores, motor vehicle and parts dealers, and clothing and clothing accessory stores. The Internet and e-commerce are transforming the world of sales and some firms have created the position of Internet sales manager to handle their Web-based sales operations.

Did You Know?

Inventory shrinkage—a combination of employee theft, shoplifting, vendor fraud, and administrative error—cost United States retailers over $31 billion last year according to the latest National Retail Security Survey report on retail theft, which analyzed theft incidents from 118 of the largest U.S. retail chains.

> ## "I am the world's worst salesman; therefore, I must make it easy for people to buy."
> —F. W. Woolworth, creator of the Woolworth's chain of "five and dime" stores

Job Seeking Tips

Follow these specific tips for retail sales managers and then turn to Appendix A for help on résumés and interviewing.

- ✔ Decide what piques your retail interest and seek work accordingly.
- ✔ Build a résumé of experiences that showcases your abilities and talents.
- ✔ Talk to the career placement office at your school.
- ✔ Gain entry-level work in a business where you would like to advance.

Interview with a Professional:
Q&A

Ray LaForge

President/retail sales manager, Olympic Outfitters,
Olympia, Washington

Q: *How did you get started?*

A: I got started in college working as a salesperson for a men's store, learning the basics of selling. I also spent a year working as a special events manager for Coca Cola, where I learned to manage a small staff and balance daily books. After college, I worked as assistant manager of my college bookstore, which afforded me solid basic training in retail management.

After acceptance in the graduate program in creative writing at the University of Montana, a good friend from college convinced me to buy and sell a small container of European derailleur bicycles, which at that time were something of a phenomenon in America. We were so successful at distributing the bikes that we decided to open a storefront selling bikes and accessories. Eventually, we added hiking, climbing, skiing, and water sports to our product mix and today, after 36 years in business, we are considered specialists in the outdoor recreational category.

Q: *What's a typical day like?*

A: A typical day begins with opening the doors. I walk the store to make sure that displays and racks are in order and that the floor is generally neat and clean. I check to see what staff levels are likely to be for the day. I print a profit margin report for the previous day, enabling me to review each individual sale. If any thing is amiss, I will make a note to discuss the particulars of that transaction with the salesperson involved. I will periodically review statements of income and expense. I also review vendor invoices to see what we owe and when we will pay it. I might update cash-flow projections. I will often spend time as a buyer or with buyers in product line showings deciding what to buy for the store. And, often, I will spend some time on the sales floor talking to and assisting customers and clients.

Q: *What's your advice for those starting a career?*

A: Get a job in a professional retail organization. Learn the basics of selling. Make sure that your job involves products you can be enthusiastic about selling. Educationally, develop your communication skills. Those who communicate have a greater degree of success than those who don't.

Do not make conclusions in advance about customers in retail. It is often surprising who has money and is willing to spend it, particularly if they are treated respectfully. Develop skills in managing, merchandising, and buying. It may lead to a career on the distribution side of retail working for a vendor.

Q: *What's the best part of your job?*

A: The best part of my job is the satisfaction I get in knowing that I may have introduced someone to an outdoor activity—skiing, biking, hiking, etc.—which could potentially benefit their lives. I also cherish being my own boss and the freedom it affords me. And, over the years I have been proud of the former employees who have gone on to create their own success stories.

Career Connections

For further information, contact:

National Retail Federation http://www.nrf.com

Retail Industry Leaders Association http://www.retail-leaders.org

Professional Retail Store Maintenance Association http://www.prsm.com

Retailchoice.com http://www.retailchoice.com

Associate's Degree Programs

Here are a few schools that offer quality programs in retail management:

Columbus State Community College, Columbus, Ohio

Burlington County College, Pemberton, New Jersey

Fashion Institute of Technology, Seattle Pacific University, Seattle, Washington

The Fashion Institute of Design and Merchandising, Los Angeles, San Francisco, Orange County, San Diego, California

Financial Aid

Some schools offer scholarship information on their Web sites and some big retailers offer their employees funding to further their education. Here are two scholarships related to retail sales. For more on financial aid for two-year students, please see Appendix B.

The **Create Your Ultimate Retail Experience Scholarship Competition** is sponsored by the Art Institute of Denver, and is designed for high school seniors interested in a career in fashion retail management. Scholarships are awarded to study fashion retail management at the Art Institute of Colorado, with the first-place prize winner receiving $3,000 and the second-place winner receiving $2,000. http://www.artinstitutes.edu/denver/

The **Robert J. Verdisco Scholarship** is for those who decide to continue their studies to pursue a bachelor's degree. The award, sponsored by the Retail Industry Leaders Association (RILA), offers a $5,000 scholarship to college and university students pursuing retail majors. http://www.retail-leaders.org

Related Careers

Buyer, regional manager, account coordinator, merchandise planner, planning analyst, assistant buyer, sales representative, showroom manager, operations manager, department manager, purchasing agent advertising, marketing manager, promotions manager, public relations manager, purchasing manager, purchasing agent, designer, colorist, stylist, studio director, mill-liaison executive, fashion executive.

Real Estate Agent/Broker

Vital Statistics

Salary: Although many professionals choose to work on a commission rather than hourly basis, the median annual earnings for real estate agents is $35,670, while real estate brokers earn a median annual salary of $58,270, including commission, according to 2006 figures from the U.S. Bureau of Labor Statistics.

Employment: The U.S. Department of Labor expects employment of sales agents and brokers to grow 9 to 17 percent from 2004 to 2014, or about as fast as the average for all occupations. Demand for workers in this field traditionally rises and falls with the ups and downs of the economy and the costs of borrowing money for home loans. As long as real estate continues to be seen as a good investment, real estate brokers and agents should be in demand.

Education: An associate's degree in real estate can be completed in two years. State requirements dictate that you be at least 18 years of age, spend a set amount of hours in class, and pass the state licensing test. Depending on your preferences, crash courses in real estate are in steady supply nationwide and can be completed in a few months. Real estate firms, however, are increasingly inclined to hire college graduates who can deal with the growing complexities of real estate sales. A good associate's degree provides instruction in the principles of business, finance, communications, marketing, advertising, and the legal aspects of real estate.

Work Environment: Cell phones and the Internet have allowed many real estate brokers and sales agents to work from their homes instead of real estate offices. Although many agents do have an office home base, agents spend a great deal of time in their "office on wheels," driving to show houses, property, or commercial space to prospective buyers.

The real estate profession is one that almost never sleeps. As you're reading this, somewhere a real estate agent is hard at work looking for houses going up for sale, playing matchmaker between a client and a property that will be somebody's Home Sweet Home; and real estate goes beyond home sales—agents deal with office space, farm land, and all types of property where people live, work, and play. In a profession with wages that can be 100 percent based on commission, transforming FOR SALE into SOLD is the name of the game.

The potential payoff is high. The median salary for the top 10 percent in the field tops $106,000. Agents earn less than brokers because they usually are independent sales workers who provide their services to a licensed real estate broker. Brokers pay agents a portion of their commission earned from the sale of a property.

Real estate people are the force behind every open house, closed sale, and erupting skyscraper—all calling cards of a profession fueled by personality, presentation, and reputation. This is a profession propelled by hustle, as more than 450,000 agents and brokers make a name for themselves marketing their abilities and reputation. You'll find ads for real estate pros in the mail, in newspapers, on TV, at bus stops, and even in flashy computer presentations in upscale restaurant bathrooms. Many advertise that they are affiliated with a nationally or locally recognized real estate franchise such as Century 21 or Weichert Realtors. Under this arrangement, the broker pays a fee in exchange for the privilege of using the name of the parent group.

Real estate commissions vary between 4 to 10 percent, depending largely on the type of property, current market conditions, and the eagerness of the seller. Although beginning agents shouldn't expect to close a sale for months, a typical 6 percent commission rate could net a cool $30,000 on a $500,000 house. Agents find a still greater commission payday in expensive housing markets such as Aspen, Colorado, or the north side of Chicago, with average home prices ranging well past a million dollars.

Anyone over the age of 18 with a high school diploma who successfully finishes a training course and passes a licensing exam can become a real estate agent; but knowledge is power and the more you know about the complexities of real estate, the further you are likely to go. Consult the Web site for the National Association of Realtors in the Career Connections section at the end of this chapter for detailed information on local requirements.

On the Job

If you're not a social creature, turn to another chapter. Successful real estate agents work closely with people selling and buying homes. When meeting with buyers, they have to get a full understanding of exactly the type of home they're looking for and how much they can afford to spend. They also spend time tracking down sellers and convincing them that they will be the best real estate agent or broker to sell their property. Agents/brokers then discuss with sellers the price they're seeking and review all the selling points—big kitchen, outdoor patio, view of the lake, four bathrooms, etc.

All these in-person meetings require a lot of moving. If you're not on the phone moving your lips, then you're moving your body to get to an appointment to talk with a client or greet guests at an open house. Typically, young real estate professionals start their career at an entry-level position with a developer or property manager, or as a sales agent's assistant. These beginner jobs give invaluable experience that can catapult you to your first sale or promotion. Plus, earning a set salary in an assistant position may be preferable to working exclusively on commission, especially while you're still getting your bearings in the business.

In addition to selling real estate owned by other people, brokers may be hired to manage or rent various properties by a property owner. Brokers can also help potential buyers obtain financing. On occasion, some real estate brokers and agents act as go-betweens for buyers and sellers, helping to negotiate property terms and prices.

A comprehensive understanding of business trends, property locations, and leasing practices is crucial when selling or leasing business property. Agents working to sell or lease industrial properties must be keenly aware about the region's utilities, health and education facilities, and labor supply. Although full-time agents may sell more properties, part-time workers have found that real estate can be a flexible way to supplement their income.

> ## "It's tangible, it's solid, it's beautiful. It's artistic, from my standpoint, and I just love real estate."
> **—Donald Trump, developer and media persona**

 ## Keys to Success

To be a successful real estate agent/broker, you will need strong:

- communication and people skills
- endurance for the occasional 12-hour day
- initiative for marketing yourself
- networking abilities
- sales and analytical skills

Do You Have What It Takes?

If a career in real estate piques your interest, you should be comfortable with being "on" most of the time. This vocation can make you feel as if you're a doctor on call, meeting clients at a moment's notice, sometimes on weekends or during hours atypical of a 9-to-5 work schedule. You can wind up discussing real estate propositions on golf courses, at social functions, and over meals. The job requires that you have reliable transportation, professional clothes, and an appetite for burning some social calories. In a profession strongly guided by communication skills and business sense, budding real estate agents/brokers can develop a "starter kit" of the requisite career tools by taking classes in speech, economics, business, marketing, and advertising. A fondness for learning comes in handy too, to keep up with developments in your field.

A Typical Day at Work

Out-of-the-ordinary days in real estate are typical. Very little runs as foreseen in a real estate agent's day. Agents may deal with a dozen potential buyers at a time, carefully scheduling visits to available properties; but meetings don't always go as scheduled, and agents have to bend to people's busy workdays.

Staying organized is essential. Realtors must be diligent file-keepers and navigate the multipage forms for the purchase agreement, paperwork for the mortgage company, and the report detailing the professional inspection of the house. Depending on how the inspection goes, you may even need to renegotiate the purchase agreement.

If by some miracle you haven't been called out of the office to attend to clients, part of your day may be dedicated to the upkeep of your presence in the community. You have to make sure you have enough brochures and fliers to keep the lawn boxes full in front of properties that are for sale. You may also update your Web site to assure it's presenting current information about your services. Making a name for yourself and marketing your neighborhood presence is a large part of developing your business.

Then there are leads. Good realtors don't rest on their last sale. Instead they scour the Internet looking for newly listed properties that could be a match for their clients. Sometimes that extra step or dash of creativity is what can make the difference. "I usually take my own photos of listings and hire companies to do panoramic type photography to put on a Web site," says Coldwell Banker real estate professional Veryle Logan Hudson.

In this profession it helps to be a Jack or Jill of all trades, whether it's developing your own promotional materials or matching up your client's financial situation with the right lender. Some buyers need assistance in handling the financial aspects of buying a home, and if you can guide them to the right information on mortgages, it may help you secure the sale.

How to Break In

Although networking is a buzzword for most aspects of employment, in real estate it is especially critical. Real estate circles can be tight, and often veterans in the field rely on word-of-mouth advice from contacts and personal networks in making their recruiting decisions. Because realtors often begin selling in their own communities, students interested in the field should take an active interest in their town. The more you know about school districts, property taxes, neighborhood shopping, and other highlights, the better you will be at selling. Young people should also try getting part-time work in a realtor's office to get a sense of what the work is like up close and establish some job networking contacts.

Job opportunities in the industry are divided into four distinct fields: sales, management, development, and acquisition and analysis. Although crossover among these sectors is possible, most people start out specializing in a specific area.

- Sellers and leasers traffic in everything from residential real estate to commercial deals involving corporations and office towers.
- Property managers are tasked with maintaining the value of a property (of course), managing finances, dealing with tenants, and providing for the physical care of the property.
- Developers are real estate dreamers who translate chalkboard ideas into life-sized reality, in a process involving engineers, zoning officials, builders, lenders, architects, and interested tenants.
- Real estate analysts specialize in understanding how to assess a property's value while trudging through the maze of zoning laws, environmental impact reports, land-use regulations, and other hurdles for the acquisition and development of property.

Two-Year Training

Although crash courses may be enough to get you over the hurdle of passing the state real estate licensing exam, transactions are becoming more legally complex. As a result, many real estate agencies tend toward hiring brokers or agents who have at least some college experience. A good two-year associate's degree program will include not only courses in real estate, but also business administration, law, finance, English, communications, statistics, and economics. Don't leave school without an understanding of how interest rates work and fluctuate. Those individuals who aspire to set up their own business could increase their chances for success with courses in accounting and marketing.

Just how much time you need to punch in for state classroom training varies widely. Those wishing to practice in Alaska or New York need 20 and 45 hours, respectively, while Washington and Georgia want a bit more of your time, requiring 60 and 75 hours of classroom time, respectively. The examination—more comprehensive for brokers than agents—includes questions on basic real estate transactions and laws affecting the sale of property. Most states require candidates for the general sales license to complete 30 to 90 hours of classroom instruction.

In addition to classroom training, potential agents and brokers would do well to look for work opportunities where they can hone and refine their communications and sales abilities. A broker's license requires 60 to 90 hours of formal training and a specific amount of experience selling real estate, usually one to three years. Some states waive the experience requirements for the broker's license for applicants who have a bachelor's degree in real estate.

Note also that the National Association of Realtors encompasses many local real estate associations that sponsor courses that cover fundamental and legal aspects pertinent to the field of real estate. The National Association of Realtors also provides advanced courses in property development, mortgage financing, management, and other subjects.

What to Look For in a School

When considering a two-year school, be sure to ask these questions:

☞ What is the success rate of their graduates in passing the state exam?

☞ How cool or hot is the real estate market relative to your school's location?

☞ How active is the school with regional or national realty organizations?

☞ Are there opportunities to assist in the offices of current realtors?

☞ Do the professors have a successful track record in selling properties?

The Future

The great thing about real estate is it's not going away. It's the level of demand and the number of jobs the market can support that will fluctuate. Qualified salespeople face plenty of competition as more people enter this field aspiring to earn big paychecks. Opportunities should grow on the management side as rental housing, apartments, condominiums, and assisted-living housing spreads. Those who want security can find work as appraisers, as these jobs are less affected by industry cycles.

Did You Know?

Jupiter Island, Florida, was named the most expensive neighborhood in America in 2003, with a median home price of $5.6 million. Aspen, Colorado, came in second with an average cost of $2.6 million per home.

Interview with a Professional: Q&A

Veryle Logan Hudson

Real estate agent, Coldwell Banker, Minneapolis, Minnesota

Q: *How did you get started?*

A: I had such a hard time finding a home when I went looking for a house, I just knew I could do better—the realtors I experienced weren't very interested in listening. I knew that I could do this job and be an exceptional listener, which is one of the most important traits a realtor can have. I like looking at homes and matching the right home to the right person.

Q: *What's a typical day like?*

A: Long, hectic, exciting. Generally not exactly as you planned it the previous day. You start out early, and your plan is to get some of your administrative or marketing work done and suddenly you get a call to go show a home. Everything is always an emergency in real estate; you have nervous buyers, nervous sellers—you end up communicating more often than you anticipated. Days never go as planned, which also makes them very exciting.

Q: *What's your advice for those starting a career?*

A: Talk to several companies while you're preparing for your real estate license exam. When you go into the offices you can gauge how helpful they will be in sharing information. You have to work out if you'll be swimming with friendly fish or fighting with difficult sharks. Also, since it is a commission business, you have to be in a position to have some reserves to handle your finances for just a few months.

Q: *What's the best part of your job?*

A: It's the joy on a person's face when they get the home that they've dreamt about and imagined themselves in. Being a part of their lives and being a part of the biggest purchase they'll ever make is remarkable.

Job Seeking Tips

Follow these tips for retail estate agents/brokers and then turn to Appendix A for help on résumés and interviewing.

✔ Select your location carefully, investigating where property sales are most plentiful.

✔ Build a résumé of work experience that showcases your people skills and entrepreneurial spirit.

✔ Inquire with brokerage, development, and management firms about internships. After you get one, be ready to take on an entry-level position. Be open and enthusiastic and exhibit your hunger for learning.

✔ Take the real estate test in your state shortly after you've completed your coursework.

✔ If you live close to a state border, consider seeking more than one license.

Career Connections

For further information, contact:

Institute of Real Estate Management http://www.irem.org/

National Association of Realtors http://www.realtor.org/

Realty Times—Real Estate News and Advice http://realtytimes.com/

Pension Real Estate Association http://www.prea.org

Associate's Degree Programs

Here are a few schools offering quality real estate agent/broker programs:

New York Real Estate Institute, New York, New York

Jefferson Community College, Louisville, Kentucky

San Juan College, Farmington, New Mexico

East Los Angeles College, Monterey Park, California

Irvine Valley College, Irvine, California

Hennepin Technical College, Minneapolis, Minnesota

Community College of Philadelphia, Philadelphia, Pennsylvania

Financial Aid

Here are a few real estate-related scholarships listed below. As a rule of thumb, it may be wise to check with your state association of realtors and inquire about what they can provide. For more on financial aid for two-year students, see Appendix B.

The **Community College Real Estate Education Endowment Fund** is for those studying real estate in California. Find out about the various educational opportunities by visiting the Chancellor's Office of California Community Colleges.   http://www.cccco.edu, or http://www.cccco.edu/divisions/ss/financial_assist/attachments/real_estate_0506/re_app_0607.pdf for the endowment fund.

Ohio Association of Realtors Scholarships is for students in that state. Contact Ruth Pitts, Ohio Association of Realtors, 200 East Town Street, Columbus, Ohio 43215 (614) 241-6675.

The **National Association of Industrial Office Parks** has many chapters that offer a $1500 scholarship in the spring to a student interested in real estate, based on financial need and academic achievement. http://www.naiop.org

The **Pension Real Estate Association Scholarships** awards tens of thousands of dollars to those who go on to pursue advanced degrees in real estate.   http://www.pres.org

Related Careers

Real estate appraiser, sales representative, property manager, investment banker, property developer, financial services representative.

Advertising Sales Agent

Vital Statistics

Salary: The median annual income for advertising sales agents is $40,300, according to 2006 data from the U.S. Bureau of Labor Statistics.

Employment: Overall projected job growth of 9 to 17 percent growth from 2004 to 2014 is in line with the average for all occupations.

Education: A certificate in management development geared toward preparing for an entry-level position in sales can be earned in as little as four months. For those who desire a broader background, associate's degree programs in marketing and sales can be completed in anywhere from 12 to 24 months. A good associate's degree for this field will touch upon the principles of marketing, marketing theory, advertising, business, professional communication, and sales techniques.

Work Environment: A typical workweek exceeds 40 hours. Most advertising sales professionals work in an office setting, but have the flexibility to determine their own schedule as long as quotas are met.

Space isn't just the final frontier, it's for sale. On billboards, in the pages of *People* magazine, on the airwaves between breaks during your favorite *Simpsons* episode. Do you think all those Taco Bell ads during the dinner hour are pure coincidence? Is it any wonder you see more advertisements for flowers, chocolate, or day retreats to the spa before Valentine's Day in your local paper? Selling advertising is about timing and demonstrating to clients why your media outlet is the perfect platform for expanding their customer base.

Advertising revenue is typically considered to be a bellwether for the health of magazines, newspapers, broadcasters, and directories. If you are part of the 50 percent of advertising sales agents in media, your role will be critical in their success. Today's advertising landscape is quickly changing and includes banner ads on the Internet, ads on cell phones, and satellite radio. Sometimes it seems like any space you can imagine has the potential to display an ad—sides of buildings, subway cars, taxis, airports, buses, shopping carts, and roadside billboards all display ads. Some sales agents specialize in selling direct mail advertisements—circulars about grocery store sales, books of coupons, and letters designed to get you to buy, buy, buy.

With quarterly sales quotas casting shadows over workers, this field isn't for the faint of heart; but for those who have a talent for sales, the earning potential is enormous. According to the Bureau of Labor Statistics, the top 10 percent of the 154,000 jobs in the industry earn more than $89,000 per year.

In this field, 30 percent of all agents in the field work in the publishing business for newspapers, periodicals, books, and directories, with 2 in 10 workers making sales calls for radio and television broadcasters. The best-paying jobs are typically found in larger media markets.

"Early to bed, early to rise, work like hell and advertise."
—Ted Turner, medial mogul, founder of cable
channels CNN and superstation WTBS

On the Job

Typically, on-the-job training is a vital component of this field even if you possess a newly minted degree and a sales track record. This isn't a field in which you hire somebody and throw him into the lake to see if he can swim. Generally, those starting out will be taken under the wing of an experienced sales manager who will do a little bit of coaching after observing a few sales calls and interactions with clients. Those who have wowed their managers with persuasive sales skills climb up the ladder to dealing with bigger, more important clients.

Regardless of whom they work for, advertising sales agents should be comfortable putting their personality on display every day. Since they are the link between their company and the client organizations (the ones making the spending decisions), advertising sales agents must have outstanding interpersonal and communications skills. Professionals in this field must be self-motivated and work independently because advertising sales agents typically set their own schedules and work without much supervision.

Agents have to enjoy working with people. They're continually on the phone or at meetings telling potential clients how they can spend their dollars to reach an audience that will increase their sales. Professionals in this field rely on an understanding of human psychology—they know what motivates people to buy. Although days can be filled with rejections, those who succeed know how to move on and maintain a positive attitude (because negativity can kill a sale).

As far as pay is concerned, an advertising sales agent takes home a combination of salary, bonuses, and commissions, with the latter, of course, being based on the amount of sales generated. Although the tension can be high in a field potentially rich in rejection or polite "no, thank yous," the privileges and perks for outstanding sales executives can be phenomenal. Top sellers can receive all-expenses-paid vacations or gifts as rewards for hitting or surpassing sales goals.

 ## Keys to Success

To be a successful advertising sales agent, you will need:

- strong organizational skills
- the ability to work independently
- multitasking abilities
- a knack for being persistent
- confidence, pure and simple
- good people skills
- the power of persuasion

> ## "The sale most often goes to the most interested party."
> —Steven Chandler, author, *100 Ways to Motivate Yourself*

Do You Have What It Takes?

Presentation, personality, and communication skills are the three major traits upon which advertising sales agents rely. You also need confidence, thick skin, and a high tolerance for stress, rejection, and the ever-present Sword of Damocles known as sales quotas. It should be said too that turnover in this field is higher than normal, as many advertising sales agents decide that commission-based earnings are too hard to depend on.

People-pleasers tend to thrive in this career because the job is often all about keeping the client happy. This is a career in which the little things can really matter. Those who buy advertising from you often want to feel you're attentive to their needs, friendly, and listening to what they want. High school students considering a career in this field should bulk up on business and communications classes. Proficiency in Spanish or another foreign language can make you a particularly sought-after candidate in an age of once-niche markets entering the mainstream, as with Hispanic and Asian-language cable television and radio. Also, creativity counts. Sales agents often must come up with clever ways to make a product stand out against the competition—from an offer to receive a free sample of a new soft drink to a scratch-and-sniff ad for a new cologne.

A Typical Day at Work

As a sales agent, most of your day is spent on the phone—calling prospects and touching base with current advertisers. Sometimes, a more personal touch is required, so you make sure you're dressed professionally and ready to meet clients in person. You try to be upbeat and optimistic even on days when you're feeling down. When you get a potential client on the phone, you turn on your powers of persuasion to convince the business why your publication or medium is the perfect place for reaching potential customers. You may stress reader or viewership numbers. Sometimes, businesses want to target a specific demographic or segment of the population that is likely to buy the product, and you can readily describe your reach— whether it be high school students or women ages 18–34. If you're selling space online, you might discuss the number of hits your site receives each day. Some of your advertisers want proof that they're getting response. At a magazine, you might have a business-reply-card promotion in which readers can reply, showing their interest in a product.

In-house, you spend time talking with people in marketing and promotions to make sure their work is supporting your sales efforts. You also consult with those in charge of content because the buyer will be interested in the editorial matter running alongside. (At a magazine, what articles are planned for upcoming issues? A new section on food may be a perfect match for restaurants to advertise in.) To write a proposal for a new client, you spend time at your computer typing up the details, including a budget going over specific costs. You might call in an art director and copywriter to help with your pitch.

Usually, you complete a status report by the end of the week, recording the contacts you've made, the potential for doing business with them, and the status of existing client contracts.

How to Break In

Two-year schools can teach the marketing, advertising, and sales techniques needed to advance in this career. Aspiring salespeople need to hone their written and oral communications as well. In high school and college, students can get sales experience working for the school newspaper, yearbook, or a student government campaign. Graduates increase their employability with knowledge of a particular niche market or some proven sales history. You can get this experience through an internship or a part-time job in the field. Agents can often gain more skills and responsibilities working in a smaller firm, and then advancing to a higher position at a bigger company.

Two-Year Training

If you feel like you have a personality suited for sales, certificate programs can be completed in as a little as a semester. However, two-year degrees in either sales and marketing or business typically provide a broader and more marketable base of education. The old adage "you get what you pay for" applies here, so do research on all schools you're considering. Find out whether graduates are working in their field.

In general, those interested in ad sales take courses in advertising, sales management technology, advertising campaigns, public speaking, business communications, accounting, promotions, and marketing. Sales agents can sink or swim on their ability to get their point across orally and in written form, so communication classes are essential. Any extracurricular training in speech or debate may help hone these skills. Consider giving preference to schools that make internships a requirement for graduation. An internship may only count for three of the 60+ credits in your program, but its value in real-world experience and the opportunity to develop connections within your field is priceless.

What to Look For in a School

When considering a two-year school, be sure to ask these questions:

☞ Does this degree program provide an internship requirement?

☞ What is the school's job placement rate?

☞ How credible are the professors? Have they worked in your field, and if so, for how long?

☞ Will your program offer targeted sales courses for your preferred area of specialization?

The Future

As the population grows, so too will money spent on advertising. As cable systems become increasingly insatiable in their appetite for new niche advertising markets encouraged by new channels, advertising sales agents will become an integral part of keeping new outlets afloat. In a country in which Spanish is the first language for many, speakers who can build from their high school knowledge base are set up for being attractive candidates in advertising as Hispanic markets continue to command an increasing portion of all media.

Interview with a Professional:
Q&A

Philip Vontron
Account manager, *Stack* Magazine, Cleveland, Ohio

Q: *How did you get started?*

A: In college, I decided I wanted to do marketing and advertising. I worked at a place called Top DJ Gear. From there, I got a job as an ad sales assistant at *Complex* magazine about hip-hop and urban culture. I had a great mentor there—Moksha Fitzgibbons. He's a workaholic. *Stack* magazine pulled me over. *Stack* provides how-to training, nutrition, and sports skills for high school athletes. We take the workouts of top professional athletes and present them for high school athletes.

Q: *What's a typical day like?*

A: I reply to e-mail and set up and go on about 10 in-person sales calls a week, or two a day. In-person meetings work better than on the phone. Sales is definitely about relationships—people liking you. Advertisers aren't used to targeting teens in print. I have to teach them that we are actually reaching their audience. I meet with media planners and buyers. I travel in the south to places like Atlanta—I love to travel. The commissions drive me. It's stressful but rewarding. The more you work, the more financial reward you get.

Q: *What's your advice for those starting a career?*

A: Decide where you want to work and really go for it. For a magazine, look at the magazine, find out the people who are in charge, and call them. Send them your résumé. Be relentless. Find a subject you like—I like sports. I get to go to games with the clients. It's fun. Start reading the trades—*Advertising Age, Media Week, Brand Week*. You have to have confidence for this career to go into meetings and pitch your product. You become a master of the marketplace you're working in, which makes you more employable. People come to you for your knowledge.

Q: *What's the best part of your job?*

A: I like that you get to meet a lot of new people. It's definitely an out-of-office job.

Did You Know?

The highest advertising rate for a television series averaged $2 million for a 30-second spot during the 2004 hour-long final episode of *Friends*.

Job Seeking Tips

Follow these specific tips for advertising sales agents and then turn to Appendix A for help on creating résumés, interviewing, and collecting references.

✔ Reach out to professional sales organizations that can help you connect to potential employers.

✔ Check on the size audience for the media you're interested in. For example, has the circulation for a publication you're applying to expanded or contracted over the last few years?

✔ Gain relevant experience in an internship. Especially look into interning in a niche area that interests you.

✔ If you have a foreign language skill to offer, ask yourself if your environment will allow you to take advantage of your bilingual asset.

✔ Investigate your school's employment resources, including the job placement office. Who recruits on campus? Are there career fairs on campus?

Career Connections

For further information, contact:

American Advertising Federation http://www.aaf.org

The Newspaper Association of America http://www.naa.org

Talent Zoo (advertising, marketing, and public relations jobs) http://www.talentzoo.com

Associate's Degree Programs

Here are a few schools offering quality programs for those wanting to become advertising sales agents:

Del Mar College, Corpus Christi, Texas

Gateway Technical College, Kenosha, Wisconsin (offers emphasis in radio broadcasting)

Brown Mackie College, 21 locations across Florida, Georgia, Illinois, Ohio, Indiana, Kansas, Kentucky, Texas, Colorado, and California

Nicolet College, Rhinelander, Wisconsin

The University of Akron, Akron, Ohio

Financial Aid

Many schools offer advertising scholarships within communications or business communications departments. Here are a few awards related to ad sales. For more on financial aid for two-year students, see Appendix B.

The **American Advertising Federation** provides a list of scholarships for students and advanced professionals alike. Look under "Career Connections."   http://www.aaf.org

The **Cleveland Ad Association** funds scholarships to deserving Ohio residents attending Ohio schools and majoring in advertising or other aspects of business communications.   http://www.clevead.com/

The **California Chicano News Media Association,** hailed as being for a "hire purpose," offers the Joel Garcia Memorial Scholarship Fund for media professionals of many ethnicities.   http://www.ccnma.org

The **John S. and James L. Knight Foundation,** as in the Knight-Ridder newspaper giant, provides numerous scholarships for media professionals.   http://www.knightfdn.org

Related Careers

Sales consultant, retail sales associate, customer service representative, marketing coordinator, client service representative, call center representative.

E-Commerce Specialist

Vital Statistics

Salary: The annual average income for e-commerce specialists is about $59,000, according to 2006 figures from the U.S. Bureau of Labor Statistics. Newcomers will need time and experience before getting enough work to make that amount.

Employment: The need for e-commerce specialists is expected to remain high as computer-related design and services are projected to remain among the fastest-growing niches of the U.S. economy.

Education: An associate's degree in e-commerce can be obtained in two years or less under the heading of business or e-business. For those already grounded in business principles, some schools offer technical certificate programs under the heading E-Commerce Specialist Certificate. A good program will emphasize aspects of e-business unique to the Internet, providing an understanding of the technical aspects of e-commerce, including how to design a secure e-commerce system and instruction on how to design Web advertising and marketing plans.

Work Environment: E-commerce specialists typically put in 40-hour workweeks in an office setting, although telecommuting is becoming more common for computer professionals as access to Wi-Fi (an abbreviation of *wireless fidelity* that refers to the operating standards for area networks and devices that use them) allow workers to be productive from remote locations. Some e-commerce specialists can expect the occasional emergency phone call if the system goes down. You've been warned.

Shop. Click. Spend $100 billion.

That's what consumers were projected to spend in 2006, according to the Internet industry watchers at comScore. An Internet without a sales angle would be as unimaginable as television without commercials. Selling via the Internet is known as e-commerce, and shopping online is no longer a holiday novelty to avoid long lines. In the MySpace, Facebook, and YouTube age, hanging out on the Internet has become just as commonplace as hanging out at the mall. E-commerce specialists are becoming some of the most important builders of the 21st century, keeping businesses and social lives running for the Internet's millions of visitors. This career combines computer and marketing skills to build Web sites that attract customers, encourage them to buy, and make the purchasing process as easy as possible. In this field, the badge "techie" is worn with honor and can pave the way to a career in which professionals at the top of their field earn six figures.

As broadband cable continues to spread throughout the world, the Travelocities, Best Buys, Amazons, *Wall Street Journals,* and ESPN.coms of the world are filled with advertising banners. Purchasing opportunities are just a click away for customers who have a credit card. Whether it's a plane ticket, a refrigerator, stock market research, DVDs, or the inside sports scoop, e-commerce is a limitless marketplace with companies selling products, information, or services. As a result, the demand is high for those who know how to use the Web as a medium for bringing a traditional store to the virtual marketplace.

E-commerce specialists have the technical and computer programming know-how to set up systems for ordering goods and services; but because those who buy online may not be so tech-savvy, the e-expert has to create Web sites that are easy to understand. They need to make purchasing a snap for the consumer. To do so, these professionals also rely on strong communications and marketing skills. Also, e-commerce professionals should have a fascination and appetite for learning new technologies. In this quickly changing world, an essential part of their job is to keep up with the latest in merchant tools, customer tracking, and design. They need to follow how other businesses are advertising online and handling online purchases.

On the Job

The role of an e-commerce expert varies from job to job. You might be setting up the system for consumers to order CDs online, allowing them to securely provide credit card and other information in making a transaction. It takes only one bad experience with credit card information to lose a customer for life, so maintaining consumer confidence and establishing a reputation as a secure storefront can be almost as valuable as the products your company sells.

Your work could also involve establishing an online catalogue of goods and setting up the advertisements on a Web site, or you could be part of a campaign to promote your site through a series of banner ads and strategically honed links.

In the land in which commerce is king, being a specialist in this field involves applying and adapting to ever-changing technology that's used to increase traffic and sales. Your typical day could include figuring out how to drive traffic to your site, while making sure you appear on the appropriate search engines and double-checking to make sure you're linked to other Web sites that will help you find potential customers.

Part of your job could include consulting with potential clients to formulate a business profile on how best to serve their e-commerce needs.

Beginners can start out as service representatives, Web site designers, account executives, marketing coordinators, or Web site administrators.

The definition of an e-commerce specialist is nearly as encompassing as the Internet itself. As advertising banners generate revenue—revenue that e-marketers measure with special tracking software—and as marketing and advertising professionals are needed for any company's online presence, anyone working for a business that sells any type of product could be asked to learn the nuts and bolts behind how their commercial site works. However, those who can really be considered specialists are the so-called techies; they are the programmers, designers, and database administrators who keep the relationship up and running between your company's online presence and your company's customers.

> **"The advance of technology is based on making it fit in so that you don't really even notice it, so it's part of everyday life."**
> —Bill Gates, founder of Microsoft

Keys to Success

To be a successful e-commerce specialist, you should have:

- strong oral and written communication skills
- an understanding of Web-based computer programming
- the ability to self-motivate
- a team-player attitude
- the capacity to build and maintain strong customer relationships
- the willingness to learn new technologies
- patience with those less versed in your field of expertise

Do You Have What It Takes?

If you spend a lot of time online and have a curiosity about Web technologies, tools, and content, this career could be for you. Students interested in e-commerce should excel at, or have great patience for, learning programs. Although many tools have been developed for making Web pages easier to build, those who advance in this field generally have more programming ability and experience. Along with mastering basic computer languages and programming, those likely to succeed have some natural sales ability. They know what motivates people to make a purchase.

A Typical Day at Work

In addition to the big goals of selling as much as possible to the world, e-commerce specialists typically are asked to assist with standards, technologies, and practices for business-to-business (known as B2B) and e-commerce models. These professionals conduct market research, interviewing existing customers to understand what motivates them and what makes purchasing online easiest for them. Part of your day may include interacting directly with customers or vendors (those whose goods you sell on your site or use to make it) via e-mail or a phone call to place an order or resolve a problem. Depending on your specialty, you could be using software tools to track products (inventory control) or customers in various databases or using your Java or html skills to make sure the Web site's virtual checkout counters (payment gateways) are in working order. You may plan a sale and send out a *broadcast* e-mail to a large database of customers announcing your special deals.

How to Break In

A two year-degree in e-commerce can certainly open doors, but to get a leg up on the competition do a little sleuthing or surfing in your local online community and find a small business to help create, design, and maintain its Web site. Alternatively, there's no shortage of nonprofit organizations seeking aspiring Internet professionals who can help improve and raise their online image. The time you volunteer now could be a down payment on developing a portfolio that wins you your first career-track internship or entry-level job.

Two-Year Training

If you have a few years of retail experience and a working knowledge of some basic business practices, an E-Commerce Specialist Certificate may be just the ticket to get you where you want to be. For those looking for a broader education or for students who are a little less versed in business basics, a good e-commerce program will provide you with the understanding to help businesses develop their presences on the Internet. E-commerce programs come in many shapes and sizes. When searching out a program in this field, keep in mind that you may find e-commerce instruction under an associate's degree heading of business, or as an associate of science under e-business. Certification programs, which are typically shorter in duration, are commonly referred to as e-commerce certificates.

A good two-year program will provide instruction in Java and other Internet tools, including HTML and XHTML, while providing instruction on how to design and develop interactive Web pages. If you're eyeing a particular market, spend whatever time you can to develop a knowledge base for the major players in the field.

What to Look For in a School

When considering a two-year school, be sure to ask these questions:

☞ Will this school provide knowledge of database concepts and Web development?

☞ Will this school provide me with a practical understanding of databases?

☞ Will this school or program provide the opportunity to take classes that will add to my understanding of business fundamentals?

☞ Where are graduates of this school working right now?

☞ How well versed are your teachers in Web-authoring tools and how much real-world business experience do they have to offer when it comes to e-commerce?

☞ Are they offering courses that teach about payment gateways and inventory control?

The Future

Competition on a local, national, and international scale will fuel the demand for those who can develop and design a commercial Internet presence for a business. As computers become more affordable and access to the Internet becomes faster and cheaper, sales via the Internet are expected to rise. A degree in e-commerce can pave the way for positions such as account executive, marketing coordinator, customer service representative, Web site administrator, or Web site designer. Those wishing to increase their future marketability would do well to pick up whatever fundamental business courses in marketing and advertising they can, as both skills translate well in the online medium.

Did You Know?

The Queen of England knighted former IBM boss Lou Gerstner in 2001 for his services to e-commerce and education. To date, no one from Amazon or eBay has received honors from Her Majesty.

Interview with a Professional:
Q&A

Joe Buffaloe

Manager of third-party business—"integration ninja"
—Amazon.com

Q: *How did you get started?*

A: I started in a warehouse of a start-up as a temp. Everyone working there had to pick up some basic computer tools. We had to get some basic UNIX skills to troubleshoot for getting things fixed. At just about any e-commerce company you're going to have to be flexible and be able to respond to technology changes quickly and gracefully. In that situation, there was opportunity for anyone who could self-educate themselves on UNIX and Linux tools. People who show the ability to adapt and learn new systems with troubleshooting and programming advance and get promoted.

Q: *What's a typical day like?*

A: In my current role there's a high level of e-mail contact, and it isn't just e-commerce. I deal with a lot of external e-mail coming in from vendors who want to sell on our platform, needing to verify that they can use our tools and submit data. This allows them to fill orders and lets us know that these things have been shipped. It's all about messaging back and forth between Amazon and the vendor. There are so many parts of the business, but the technological part is involved in everything we do. Whether it's dealing with customer service or merchants, you're using software tools because all of our data is in the virtual world. Our store is really just an online portal; in everything we get done, we have to rely on data sources (such as databases) and troubleshoot them as necessary; that's why having good basic technical knowledge is valuable in any e-commerce role.

Q: *What's your advice for those starting a career?*

A: Seek out a younger company. It will give you a chance to work on things within a small scope; it will give you give a chance to work on things that will have a large impact on your workplace and improve your chances for moving on to your Microsofts and your Amazons.

Q: *What's the best part of your job?*

A: The best part is that it's constantly changing. There are a lot of new challenges that come with competition, as technology emerges to try to do things in a different way. You have to be pretty flexible to respond to changes quickly and have a good overall fix for a problem that's not going to be outdated in a year.

Job Seeking Tips

Follow these specific tips for e-commerce specialists and then turn to Appendix A for help on creating résumés, interviewing, and collecting references.

- ✔ If you find an industry or economic sector particularly attractive, it's never too early to start doing research.
- ✔ Talk to the career placement office.
- ✔ If you've designed or been a part of other Web sites, develop a portfolio exhibiting your style and talent.

Career Connections

For further information, contact:

Internet.com http://www.internet.com

Red Herring http://www.redherring.com

The Industry Standard http://www.thestandard.com

Women's E-commerce Association International http://www.wecai.org

eBusiness Association http://ebusinessassociation.org

Associate's Degree Programs

Here are a few schools offering quality two-year e-commerce or e-business programs:

Cascadia Community College, Bothell, Washington

Penn Foster College, online at http://www.pennfostercollege.edu

California College of San Diego, San Diego, California

Colorado Technical University, Colorado Springs, Colorado

Financial Aid

Here are a few e-commerce-related scholarships. Your best bet may be simply to go to Google and type in *e-commerce* or *e-business* and *scholarship*, plus your state or the name of the major city nearest to you, because many colleges offer a scholarship or two specific to the pursuit of an e-commerce education. For more on financial aid for two-year students, please see Appendix B.

The **Catalogue and E-Commerce Club of Northern California** offers a $5,000 scholarship for Bay Area (San Francisco, Oakland, and surrounding area) residents wishing to pursue studies in the fields of direct and/or interactive marketing.   http://www.cecnc.com/education.html

Northern Virginia Community College provides an "e-commerce Student Scholarship." http://www.nvcc.edu/foundation/scholarship.htm

The **Computer Associates and eBusiness Association Scholarship** from the eBusiness Association (eBA) of Upstate New York awards two $1,500 merit-based scholarships to an outstanding undergraduate student attending a local academic institution or a high school senior with plans to attend an institution in the qualified geographic area. The recipients of this award exhibit strong academic achievement, leadership skills, and thoughtful vision in the eBusiness arena. http://www.ebusinessassociation.org

Related Careers

Internet ad sales representative, Internet business developer, user interface designer, Web designer, Webmaster, Internet marketing associate, Internet product manager, Internet programmer, and information architect.

Merchandise Manager

Vital Statistics

Salary: The median annual salary for purchasing agents, excluding farm buyers, is $43,730, according to 2006 figures from the U.S. Bureau of Labor Statistics. Typically agents start as trainees for a period of one to five years, and agents may advance to become purchasing, or merchandise, managers, whose median annual income in $72,450.

Employment: According to the Bureau of Labor Statistics, 43 percent of those working as buyers and in related careers worked in the wholesale trade and manufacturing industries, and another 12 percent worked in retail trade. The remainder worked mostly in service establishments, such as hospitals, or different levels of government. A small number were self-employed. Due to diminishing employment in the manufacturing sector, job growth overall for purchasing agents is forecast to be slower than the average for all jobs through 2014, according to the bureau.

Education: An associate's degree in merchandise management can be completed in as little as 18 months. Some basic business courses in accounting, economics, marketing, and advertising provide essential training and knowledge.

Work Environment: A merchandise manager may be employed either in wholesale or in a department store or specialty retail environment. These professionals often work in a comfortable office setting and clock in a workweek that occasionally surpasses the standard 40 hours. A moderate amount of time on the road for visiting suppliers or conferences is standard.

See that Wal-Mart store out your window? Okay, maybe not right now, but you will later. Whether it's Macy's, The Gap, The Body Shop, Electronics Boutique, or Bed Bath & Beyond, it's not uncommon to pass another branch of the store you just left on the way home. Retail is everywhere, ringing up annual revenues approaching $4 trillion, according to the Bureau of Labor Statistics. To a large degree, the success of a retail outlet falls on the shoulders of the merchandise managers who determine what products to stock and how much to have on hand.

Merchandise managers juggle the past, present, and future. Their analysis of past sales and current purchasing trends helps them place orders for future items. Was there a run on rabbit-shaped soap dishes before Easter last year? Better make sure enough is in stock. Did cards, gifts, and sweaters for Grandparent's Day sell poorly last year? Maybe order a little less for this year. What colors are everywhere in fashion magazines? Mauve? Forest green? Better order more clothes in those colors for spring.

Merchandise managers make decisions like these each day. They observe their consumer base and culture at large to figure out what's hot and what's not. At the heart of it all, the merchandise manager is a retail sociologist who anticipates consumer preferences and with the wave of a magic wand—or more likely a keyboard connected to a spreadsheet—he or she can evaluate and ensure that stock is on hand when needed.

Merchandise managers typically start as buyers. As purchasing professionals, their reputations rest upon the ability to weigh costs versus quality—all the while considering availability, reliability, and general support of suppliers. A manager's goal is much the same as a consumer's. The manager wants to get high-quality goods and services at the lowest cost possible.

Managers don't just stake their livelihoods on delivering a best guess. There's a method to all of this. It can require the expertise of a team of purchasing managers, buyers, and purchasing agents who pore over inventory levels and sales records. They may turn to the team to figure out how to get the best custom-made products or resolve quality issues. In the end, if consumers are rushing into stores to buy products and profits are rising, then merchandise managers are doing their job right.

On the Job

Day to day, merchandise managers rely on keen analytical skills. They are constantly evaluating their sales history and consumer trends in an effort to help their company improve business. Along with detailed analysis, managers rely on self-confidence and a willingness to take risks based on their research.

When it comes times for ordering products to sell, merchandise manages have to be good at sizing up suppliers. Are the products the best quality for the price? Will the commodity be delivered on time? Any delay can bring a firm to a screeching halt and end up costing customers and reputation.

Managers depend on computers for analysis and tracking sales. Also, the Internet can be a useful tool to research potential suppliers—reading about them in trade journals, catalogues, and publications.

Merchandising is a collaborative effort. These professionals work closely with the promotions, marketing, and advertising departments within an organization to plan what items will be on sale—just as your suppliers have a multilevel process in planning how best to appeal to you. Merchandisers also may consult with floor managers to establish where products will be positioned in a store and ensure that they are properly displayed. When it comes time to order items for sale, they turn to a distribution manager who will coordinate the delivery of goods.

A good starting point for the field is as an assistant buyer. In this role, you learn to write orders, deal with vendors, and, perhaps most importantly, how to operate within a budget. Keeping track of demand and trends is the name of the buying game.

Regardless of credits and degrees earned, aspiring merchandise professionals must demonstrate that they are cut from managerial cloth by showing their ability to handle suppliers. The job often demands fine-tuned negotiation skills to communicate with manufacturers and get the best deals.

> **"Wealth is in applications of mind to nature; and the art of getting rich consists not in industry, much less in saving, but in a better order, in timeliness, in being at the right spot."**
> —Ralph Waldo Emerson, essayist

Keys to Success

To be a successful merchandise manager, you should have:
- strong interpersonal skills
- quick and confident decision-making skills
- strong data-analysis skills
- an eye for consumer preferences
- an ability to take risks
- strong problem-solving skills

Do You Have What It Takes?

Students interested in merchandising should have a passion for two things: trends and people—the focal points for retail landscapes around the world. Courses in psychology, sociology, marketing, and communications will provide the foundation you'll need for keeping tabs on the current social climate and its impact on current consumer trends.

A Typical Day at Work

Your average day as a merchandise manager can be action packed and pressure filled. It can begin with a morning meeting with a vendor, discussing the assortment of products you may want for the upcoming season, reviewing costs, and putting in your order. You feel confident that you've ordered the right amounts and assortment based on your analysis of previous sales and current customer habits. Then, you meet with the advertising team to discuss which newspapers you'll be placing advertisements in on the weekend. Together, you review which items are being highlighted. Because you happen to be in charge of young adult clothing, you're also gearing up for the back-to-school months, and already plotting product displays and developing ideas for those ad campaigns. You have a little time at the end of the day with your trade magazines and your bookmarked retail sites as you sip a cool soda and read up on the latest trends and up-and-comers in the industry. You regularly prospect for fresh products and suppliers in your quest to find items that will please your customers and are available at a reasonable cost.

How to Break In

Retail experience is certainly a good foundation for this career, so you might try to pick up a summer or part-time job selling items that interest you—whether they be sporting goods, guitars, ice cream sundaes, etc. That part-time job could get you that reference, work experience, and networking you need to land your first full-time gig. Working in a department store, for example, can give you an insider's view into customer habits and what products sell or don't sell.

Many retailers also offer internships that can develop into full-time positions as assistant buyers or gain you entry into a firm's management-training program. Once you've paid your dues as an assistant or completed a store-sponsored management-training program, the training wheels are off, and you can become a full-fledged buyer. Internships are often available as part of associate's degree programs, which also teach you the merchandising essentials in the classroom.

Two-Year Training

Two-year associate's degree programs in merchandising provide a broad curriculum of business courses that will allow you to begin your career. Most two-year programs will connect you to possible employers as well. Classes in merchandising focus on forecasting and interpreting consumer demand. Supporting courses include economics, accounting, marketing, and statistics. Students generally must familiarize themselves with the latest software for tracking inventory. If you are drawn to any area of retail—be it farm equipment, skateboards, or high fashion—get some experience by interning or working part time in the area of your interest. An associate's degree combined with hands-on experience will make you a stronger candidate when applying for your first job.

What to Look For in a School

When considering a two-year school, be sure to ask these questions:

☞ Does the school specialize in areas or that niche market that interests me?

☞ Will the course ground me in the principles of store management?

☞ What sort of industry experience do these professors have?

☞ What internships are available and what is the school's job placement rate?

The Future

As with most professions today, the world of retail has been dramatically changed by the Internet. As e-commerce has grown, more professionals in this field have to be up to speed with selling online. Managers can also do a lot of market research via the Internet and turn to the Web for networking and for assistance from planning and distribution organizations. Retailers will continue to depend on the expertise of merchandise managers to target customers and generate sales, but if you want to be one, it's a good idea to know your way around a browser and other software.

Did You Know?

Spending 10 minutes in every store in the Mall of America would take a shopper more than 86 hours.

Job Seeking Tips

Follow these specific tips for merchandise managers, then turn to Appendix A for help on creating résumés, interviewing, and collecting references.

✔ Decide what facet of business plays to your natural talents and build on that.

✔ Figure out what kind of business or industry interests you, and develop your portfolio or work on building expertise in that field.

✔ Talk to the career placement office, preferably before graduation day.

Interview with a Professional:
Q&A

Candice Radin

Planning analyst/merchandiser, DSW Shoes,
Columbus, Ohio

Q: *How did you get started?*

A: I have always had a passion for numbers, business, and fashion, which is why I decided to major in fashion merchandising at Kent State University. Before I came to DSW Shoes, I was a store planner at Dots, Incorporated, for four and a half years where I started as a merchandise distributor. After about a year, I was promoted to store planner where I was responsible for the allocations of my product area as well as being responsible for analyzing the stores, creating and maintaining store and assortment plans, training merchandise distributors, and communicating with district and regional managers.

Q: *What's a typical day like?*

A: In my current role, I manage 150 SKUs, or stock-keeping units. I'm responsible for tracking and monitoring these styles on a weekly basis and making sure we have the appropriate inventory amounts for their sales. Every week I reforecast the sales and inventories, while working very closely with my buyer to make sure he moves around any necessary orders as well as cancel and place additional orders. I also spend a lot of time analyzing these SKUs and taking the right actions to maximize the business.

Q: *What's your advice for those starting a career?*

A: The fashion and retail industry is not as glamorous as a lot of people may think. It can be very challenging at times. If planning and allocation is the career path you want to take, you must be very numbers oriented. All positions on this side of the business work with numbers on a daily basis, so it is very important to have excellent analytical skills. If you want to progress within your career, I think one of the most important things to help you be successful is a sense of initiative. You have to want to learn the business to be successful.

Q: *What's the best part of your job?*

A: Probably the best part of my job is being responsible for so many different shoes. It's very exciting when I see how they have performed at the plans I have given them. I also really enjoy visiting stores to see what the analyzed product actually looks like at store level.

Career Connections

For further information, contact:

National Association General Merchandise Representatives http://www.nagmr.org/

Shop.org http://www.shop.org

Retail Industry Leaders Association http://www.retail-leaders.org

Association of Golf Merchandisers http://www.agmgolf.org/

International Textile and Apparel Association http://www.itaaonline. org

Associate's Degree Programs

Here are a few schools offering quality sales and merchandising associate's degree programs:

Weber State University, Ogden, Utah

Rochester Community and Technical College, Rochester, Minnesota

International Academy of Design and Technology, Chicago, Illinois

Los Angeles Trade Tech College, Los Angeles, California

Lehigh Valley College, Center Valley, Pennsylvania

Financial Aid

See below for one merchandising-related scholarship. Many community colleges offer scholarships specific to the field of retail, which is a component of merchandising. For more on financial aid for two-year students, please see Appendix B.

The **Pohle Scholarship for Retail Management/Business Administration** is offered to those who wish to pursue merchandising via a retail management route at the Community College of Rhode Island. http://www.ccri.edu

Related Careers

Purchasing specialist, purchasing manager, buyer, wholesale buyer, purchasing agent, purchasing director, purchasing manager, contract specialist, department manager, sales manager, market analyst, sales associate, assistant buyer.

Distribution Manager

Vital Statistics

Salary: The median annual earnings for purchasing agents and buyers is about $43,000, while the median earnings of those who have worked their way up to purchasing, or distribution, managers earn $72,000 per year, according to 2006 figures from the U.S. Bureau of Labor Statistics.

Employment: The field of distribution or supply chain management is a career largely in step with the manufacturing sector and the health of the economy. As the economy expands and new products and markets are developed, there will be opportunity for those who possess the technical and communications abilities necessary for understanding and managing all aspects of transforming raw materials into finished products. Prospective job seekers should keep in contact with placement offices for keeping tabs on which sectors are experiencing the most growth. The Bureau of Labor Statistics forecasts slower than average job growth overall in this field relative to other occupations.

Education: An associate's degree in management technology with an emphasis in distribution or supply chain management can be completed in as little as 24 months. A solid associate's degree program will provide instruction in the principles of business, economics, and communications. Certificate programs also are available in this field.

Work Environment: Distribution managers generally work standard hours from Monday to Friday in offices or warehouses. Some jobs involve evenings, weekends, shifts, and on-call duties.

Have you ever been to a completely empty national chain or major department store? Of course you haven't. Day in day out, throngs of consumers descend upon music stores, clothing shops, and supermarkets, and with few exceptions (for example, air conditioners during a heat wave) the shelves remain mostly stocked. How do the stores stay filled with CDs, electronics, clothes, groceries, etc.? Thank the distribution manager who makes sure that goods and materials are delivered to the stores.

Distribution managers are a critical link in a store's supply chain. That's why they are sometimes called logistics or supply chain managers. They make sure the right amount of product gets delivered to the right place at the most economically efficient cost. Logistics specialists are critical to businesses from small firms to Fortune 500 businesses. In fact, the Council for Supply Chain Management Professionals says that logistics is the second largest employment sector in the United States.

Relying on strong math and business skills, distribution managers work with massive amounts of product to determine the best routes and transportation methods to ship materials from warehouses to retail stores. Regardless of the product that's being moved, professionals in distribution have to work closely with purchasing officers and warehouse and transport managers to keep the goods moving. Using computers, these managers track how much product is available at outlets. Coordinating with purchasing agents, distribution managers then assist with reordering goods and manage the packaging and shipping of the materials. They are always concerned with improving efficiency and developing new ways to improve the delivery of product.

There is a demand for top-quality logistics professionals at all levels, including analysts, line supervisors, sales professionals, managers, directors, and vice presidents. Salaries range from less than $30,000 for entry-level positions to the compensation of senior executives who earn well into six figures.

On the Job

Descriptions of jobs in supply chain management vary greatly, and although an understanding of supply and demand is the cornerstone of this profession, job titles are not always consistent. Efficient distribution of your company's product is the name of the game. In a nutshell, as distribution or logistics manager, your primary responsibilities will involve packaging, warehouse storage, inventory, customer service, traffic management of your transportation fleet, and possibly handling aspects of the manufacturing of your product.

To get the job done right, you'll need to rely on your staff—clerical, administrative, and warehouse workers. The work often involves:

- Liaising with other professionals, such as purchasing officers and transport managers
- Learning U.S. Department of Transportation requirements and regulations
- Using computers to monitor stock levels, reorder goods, and track the movement of goods
- Analyzing and developing networks and systems for efficiency
- Managing administrative and warehouse staff

Regardless of title and starting point, supply chain managers and distributors need to develop sharp presentation and articulation skills that can be understood by a wide array of audiences. Because you may be working side by side with people from a wide array of cultural and economic backgrounds, your ability to relate and communicate in a diverse setting will go a long way toward establishing your success in this field.

Keys to Success

To be a successful distribution or supply chain manager, you should have:

- strength
- an eye for quality
- communication skills
- organizational and planning skills
- ability to understand the roles of coworkers
- capacity to interact with people from diverse backgrounds
- problem-solving skills
- computer literacy
- motivational and management skills

A Typical Day at Work

A typical day for a distribution or supply chain management professional may encompass a variety of duties. If you were working as the distribution manager for a sporting goods chain, you might start the day checking inventory and consulting with floor staff and the retail or merchandising managers at different outlets. Based on their assessment, you can determine how much product is on the shelves and how much needs to be shipped. Reviewing historical and seasonal trends, you can determine demand for specific items. When fall is coming, footballs and soccer balls have to line the shelves. As spring and summer come around, the baseball gloves and gear for water sports better be available. After you review inventory at the retail stores, you check in with your transportation manager to ensure that items are being loaded and shipped out on time. You also have to be a morale booster with your immediate staff, keeping administrative and physical laborers motivated

Because your company needs help every now and again, you also deal with third-party logistics providers, which are simply businesses that offer warehousing, packaging, staffing, and carrier services at times when you need to move more product than your set-up will allow. Besides making sure product is heading out to the consumer, you have to make sure product is coming into the warehouse. That's why you're often on the phone with manufacturers checking that goods are in the pipeline to meet your demand. You also don't want to over-order, because if you overstock you're ordering more than is being bought and your company could suffer a loss of profit.

Do You Have What It Takes?

Students interested in distribution and supply chain management should be good at math, and they shouldn't be afraid to roll up their sleeves and get a little physical at first. After all, an entry-level job could require you to physically load and unload materials as you pay your dues and learn a little about the duties required of those who work in the trenches. To that end, distribution and supply chain managers must have an interest in learning how a company operates on all levels. While in high school, aspiring distribution and supply chain managers can start plotting their course by taking as many business classes as possible. Coursework in communications can build your skills as an effective communicator who can be at ease addressing any number of audiences. Ability in a foreign language will further broaden your options as workforces across North America increasingly comprise speakers of a variety of languages, and the field of supply management is by nature global.

How to Break In

Formal qualifications are not always required, but increasingly entrants have a higher education in subjects such as logistics and supply chain management. In fact, many enter this field with an associate's degree in supply chain management. To advance in the field, you may be required by an employer to earn a graduate degree in management/procurement or supply chain management.

For many, working as an assistant distribution center manager or transportation clerk is a starting point in this field. Even unloading and loading trucks can give you insight into the career.

Record keeping and inventory tracking are both large parts of the job, so students looking to increase their marketability should become acquainted with enterprise resource planning software packages such as SAP or i2, as well as truck-routing and scheduling software such as Roadnet.

Getting involved in the on-campus business school associations and supply chain management associations listed below may help lay the groundwork for your first internship or apprenticeship. That type of real-world experience goes a long way when trying to land a first job.

Although a working knowledge of computers is standard for anyone pursuing an associate's degree, computer literacy is especially crucial in supply chain management. Unlike real estate, certification isn't required but can come in handy in a tough job market. For those already established in business or for those with less than two years' time to commit to earning an associate's degree, common certifications in this profession are Certification as a Purchasing Manager (CPM) and Certification in Production and Inventory Management (CPIM).

Two-Year Training

Often referred to by schools as management technology or logistics and supply chain management, two-year associate's degree programs in distribution provide a balanced education made up of management basics with a particular concentration in negotiation, purchasing, logistics and materials, and inventory management. A foundation in these courses empowers students with the talents needed to manage the logistics and supply chain functions of any company. In addition to business and communications basics, an associate's program will develop a student's information technology skills. On-the-job training can build a more specific knowledge of truck routing, negotiating strategies, and inventory tracking. Those students who start college having had some significant business experience may be eligible to earn experiential credit. They may also earn credit through a portfolio presentation.

What to Look For in a School

When considering a two-year school, be sure to ask these questions:

☞ Will I gain knowledge of U.S. Department of Transportation requirements?

☞ Will the school provide a background in business basics?

☞ Will I learn all the IT and software skills required for tracking business operations?

☞ Does the school provide the area of specialization I want?

☞ What business world experience do my professors have? Are they academics and researchers, or have they left the field I'm interested in?

☞ What internships are available and what is the school's job placement rate?

☞ Is the school located in a part of the country where I could see myself working?

The Future

Supply chain management is emerging from the shadows to become one of the competitive differentiators of the future, according to *Retailspeak Magazine*. As the manufacturing sector goes, so goes the need for distribution management positions. Prospective job seekers would do well to keep tabs on which industries are experiencing the most growth. Those who seek opportunity in distribution and supply chain management are at the same time making themselves viable candidates for the business world at large. The ability to manage the flow of goods requires a combination of skills that is well suited to many leadership positions.

Interview with a Professional:
Q&A

Erik van Allen

Senior director of operations, purchasing, manufacturing, warehouse, assembly, and shipping, Getman Underground Mining Equipment, Kalamazoo, Michigan

Q: *How did you get started?*

A: I went back to school to get a degree in business. While I was there, I took a class in supply chain management. That's how I ended up in the field. I got a job starting as a consultant, which exposed me to a great number of things. I was consulting in the field of strategic sourcing—acting as the interface between purchasing and inventory control. I would negotiate contracts, set up buy plans and strategies on how to buy that particular commodity.

Q: *What's a typical day like?*

A: I don't have a typical day. Part of my day involves reviewing purchasing requests from my team to see if their needs are being met. Part of my day involves working with floor supervisors and making sure that sales orders get shipped out on time, all the while monitoring where we are in terms of our building schedule which involves my supervisor team. My day also involves a lot of sales and engineering related to new truck sales or those that are on their way to completion. We do a lot of custom design. Whenever a new order comes in, there's work related to sales and it involves putting in a production schedule.

Q: *What's your advice for those starting a career?*

A: I would say, know what you like to do before you get started. If you've done some soul searching, find a career that fits. In the field of distribution and supply chain management, you need to have a strong understanding of what each of the functions of the supply chain do, regardless of where you end up. Whatever facet of the company you go into, you'll be dealing with the other ones. You'll be more effective if you appreciate what the other folks in the supply chain are trying to accomplish.

Q: *What's the best part of your job?*

A: I think you get a much broader view of a company. What you do has a very real direct impact on the success of the company, which isn't true for every job.

Did You Know?

A typical Wal-Mart distribution center spans more than one million square feet, or the equivalent of 10 Wal-Mart retail stores, and is equipped with 250 dock doors to serve the Wal-Mart fleet of trucks.

Job Seeking Tips

Follow these specifics tips for supply chain managers/distributors, and then turn to Appendix A for help on creating résumés, interviewing, and collecting references.

✔ Decide what facet of business plays to your natural talents and build on that.

✔ Figure out what kind of business or industry interests you and work on building expertise in that field.

✔ Talk to the career placement office at your school, preferably before graduation day.

> **"Wealth, like happiness, is never attained when sought after directly. It comes as a by-product of providing a useful service."**
> —Henry Ford, automaker and industrialist

Career Connections

For further information, contact the following organizations.

Council of Supply Chain Management Professionals
http://www.cscmp.org

Supply Chain Council   http://www.supply-chain.org/cs/root/home

The Stanford Global Supply Chain Management Forum
http://www.stanford.edu/group/scforum/

Jobs in Logistics Transportation/Distribution/Logistics
http://www.jobsinlogistics.com

Institute for Supply Management   http://www.ism.ws/

Women in Logistics http://www.womeninlogistics.org

Associate's Degree Programs

Here are a few schools offering quality management technology and distribution/supply chain management programs:

Post University, Danbury, Meriden, Waterbury, Connecticut

Indiana University, Kokomo, Kokomo, Indiana

Clark State Community College, Springfield, Ohio

Texas State Technical College, Waco, Texas

Highline Community College, Seattle, Washington

Metropolitan Community College, Omaha, Nebraska

Financial Aid

Here are a few distribution-related scholarships. For more on financial aid for two-year students, please see Appendix B.

Roundtable Scholarships sponsored by the Council of Supply Chain Management Professionals offer financial aid for students either on the undergraduate or graduate level in furthering their major in either logistics or supply chain management. Information on these scholarships can be found in quarterly editions of the *Educational Newsletter ed-Link,* which may be found at   http://www.cscmp.org/Website/Education/Edlink.asp.

ISM-NAPM Education Scholarships are available from the various chapters of the Institute of Supply Chain Management and the National Association of Purchasing Managers listed on the Institute of Supply Management Web site. To access scholarship information, visit and click through the links as illustrated below to get to the scholarship page: ISM homepage _ Education _ Scholastic Opportunities _ Scholarships Offered by Affiliates, Groups and Forums. It may sound like *Raiders of the Lost Distribution Scholarship,* but it's just a few clicks to a nationwide list of financial aid opportunities in the field. http://www.ism.ws

The **Annual Women in Logistics Scholarship Competition** annually awards two $1,500 scholarships to WIL members (men or women) who are pursuing an undergraduate or graduate degree in a field relevant to logistics or supply chain management at an institution in the greater San Francisco Bay Area. Applications are typically due by November 15 of each year.   http://www.womeninlogistics.org

Related Careers

Production analyst, line supervisor, sales professional, facilities manager, fleet manager, inventory specialist, materials manager, process engineer, procurement analyst, logistics analyst, process engineer, account specialist, supply chain consultant, production manager, purchasing manager, supply chain analyst, and transportation manager.

Promotions Manager

Vital Statistics

Salary: Annual salaries for junior promotion managers begin at about $33,000, according to 2006 data from the U.S. Bureau of Labor Statistics. Senior promotions managers with a breadth of skills and long experience make more than $63,000 annually.

Employment: Jobs in the promotions field are highly sought after and competition is high, but projections are for the industry to grow by 18 to 26 percent from 2004 through 2014, much faster than the rate for all other occupations.

Education: An associate's degree in sales and marketing with an emphasis in promotions is typically completed in 24 months. A good associate's degree program will provide instruction in the principles of marketing, advertising, sales, and, if your concentration is music, radio and music industry studies.

Work Environment: A promotions manager typically works in an office, but depending upon the industry (i.e., tourism or music), she or he may often work out of a hotel room while on the road since travel is sometimes required to meet clients or media representatives.

Earn an extra night's stay at a Florida hotel. Save $750 on a new Toyota. Win free groceries for a week at the local supermarket. Buy the first pair of designer jeans and get the second pair for half off! What do all these ideas have in common? They are all examples of promotions that are designed to stimulate sales, and they are all ideas dreamed up by promotions managers.

Promotions managers in the retail world are professionals who are dedicated to raising awareness through the use of incentives. With product awareness and customer retention as a goal, promotions managers direct programs that advertise incentives designed to increase sales.

While many promotions experts hustle to push retail products and establishments such as restaurants, others in this field promote musical acts, entertainers, and travel destinations. Music promoters, for example, may work for a record company or represent artists. They set up interviews with the press, television, and radio stations. They can help arrange advertising, concerts, in-store appearances, and album and ticket giveaways—anything to promote the band.

A main tool of the promoter, incentives come in a wide assortment of discounts, gifts, rebates, coupons, sweepstakes, contests, and more. Sometimes promoters organize special kickoff events or get celebrities to endorse a product. Traditionally, promotions people announce their programs through print and broadcast media as well as in-store advertising, direct mail, and catalogues; but the rapid growth of the Internet has yielded even more avenues through which promoters put their message across. Also, relatively new media such as satellite, radio, and cable television have provided additional means for reaching the public.

This field is very closely related to jobs in advertising, public relations, and marketing, and there is often a lot of overlap in these career categories. (Advertising execs may handle promotions, just as promotions managers may take care of advertising programs.) According to the Bureau of Labor Statistics, more than 64,000 advertising and promotions managers are working in the United States and earning a substantial annual income. Statistics show the average salary at $63,000 a year. Jobs in the entertainment industry are particularly sought after. Those who land the best positions generally have an extensive knowledge of the industry they're entering and have built up experience working internships and related part-time jobs.

On the Job

Similar to public relations experts, promotions professionals have strong communications and organizational skills. A talent for logistics and planning is vital. Music industry managers, for example, schedule tours and promotional activities months in advance. They try to get their artists maximum exposure, often booking them to appear on morning radio and TV talk shows, make in-store appearances, and then perform concerts at night as they tour across the country. Precision planning like this is required to promote cars, CDs, travel packages, and other products as well. This job demands strong communications skills and the ability to work well with others.

As a promotions expert, you often collaborate with other sales and marketing pros to develop programs. Speaking with media outlets is vital to reaching the widest possible audience regarding your product or service. No matter what your area of specialization is, you rely on an innovative, creative mind to think up new and exciting ways to attract consumers. You thrive on working with others—collective brainstorming with marketing and advertising departments often generates the best ideas for reaching a target audience. (Your clever slogan for the new skateboard shop could be part of a winning promotional campaign.)

Many beginners in this field work in administrative roles and handle more mundane promotional chores—visiting local merchants with product samples, leaving coupon books, stapling fliers to telephone poles, or selling T-shirts and compact disks at a merchandise booth at a concert. To get a toe in at a marketing department, you may volunteer to take on a less desirable promotional task like suiting up in a six-foot tall inflatable coffee-cup costume and giving out coupons on a busy street during rush hour.

Keys to Success

To be a successful promotions manager, you should have:
- ⚷ communication skills
- ⚷ a high energy level
- ⚷ creativity
- ⚷ an ability to connect with people
- ⚷ a knack for planning and scheduling

Do You Have What It Takes?

Those interested in a career as a promoter should excel at and enjoy courses in communications, marketing, and advertising. You need to have a true creative spark and understand the potential of creativity to motivate people. You thrive working in groups and have the flexibility needed to travel occasionally and put in long hours from time to time. An ability to relate to a diverse set of tastes and cultural backgrounds is also helpful.

A Typical Day at Work

How you spend your day could depend a great deal on the person, place, or thing you promote. Although that which is promoted will vary, how and when you target your audience will always be vital. If you're talking about promotions in the music industry, you could spend a great deal of your day on the phone or sending e-mails to arrange interviews with the press, television, and radio stations. If you're promoting a city or state, your job may be to figure out what media markets outside your city make the most sense for delivering your message. For example, an ad targeting northerners for travel to Florida and Disneyland isn't going to be very effective in the middle of a heat wave in July. Figuring out the how and when can be just as important as figuring out what your marketing message is. These are the types of decisions made by promotions professionals on a daily basis.

To generate ideas that will grab customers, you often meet with others in your company to bounce around ideas and develop sales strategies. When a strategy is agreed upon, you write up how your promotional portion should be implemented, considering staffing, budget, timing, and overall design.

How to Break In

While completing an associate's degree, aspiring promoters would do well to gain experience in an industry they would like to promote. Check with businesses locally to see if there is part-time work in their sales or public relations departments. Internships can connect you to hands-on training and provide strong networking for future employment. While in school, take advantage of opportunities to work collaboratively and get involved in promoting school events. Creating posters for a school concert, organizing a fund-raiser car wash, and helping with a student government election are all ways to build skills related to this career.

Two-Year Training

A two-year associate's degree program in sales and marketing with a concentration in promotions will develop skills for beginning a career and netting an entry-level job. Typical instruction includes advertising, marketing research, media relations, promotional campaign organization, and the computer skills needed for keeping up with related online technology. Basic media studies courses are essential as well—the career depends on your ability to communicate and persuade media outlets to help promote your product or client. Two-year programs typically have an internship element that you should take advantage of. Landing an entry-level position depends largely on making contacts and networking, which internships provide.

> ## "Without promotion, something terrible happens. Nothing!"
> **—P.T. Barnum, showman**

What to Look For in a School

Depending on what you're looking to promote, geographic location can be critical in picking a school. If you're looking for a career in travel, consider a school that's in a touristy area like San Francisco, Las Vegas, Orlando, or New York City, rather than, say, Cawker City, Kansas, where the featured attraction is the world's largest ball of twine. (Go to Cawker to learn farming.) For those looking at music promotion, check proximity to cities with thriving music scenes and small labels that are looking to promote their artists.

When considering a two-year school, be sure to ask these questions:

☞ Does the school specialize in the areas of promotions that interest me?

☞ What is the school's job placement rate? Where are their graduates working now?

☞ What are the internships like?

☞ Is the school located in a city that will give me the work opportunities I seek?

☞ What industry experience do the teachers have? Will they have stories to tell of their work in the field?

The Future

Prompted by intense domestic and global competition in offering products and services to consumers, the employment of promotions professionals is expected to increase from 18 to 26 percent from 2004 through 2014. As there are some similarities in the skills needed, professionals in the promotions field may find they also have the tools necessary to find work in marketing, advertising, or public relations. In a perpetually changing media environment, promotions managers have to keep up with the latest trends involving the Internet, satellite television, radio, and print.

Did You Know?

Promotions can backfire. A radio station in Australia planned to give away a large sum of money to one lucky winner. The plan was to drop ping-pong balls from a helicopter on a crowd and whoever found the ball with the winning number written on it would win. When the helicopter dropped the balls they all got sucked into the blades and shredded.

Job Seeking Tips

Follow these specific tips for promotions specialists, and then turn to Appendix A for help on creating résumés, interviewing, and collecting references.

✔ Build marketable skills with an internship.

✔ Promotions experts are needed in many different industries—music, travel, restaurants, sporting goods, and more. Decide which industries appeal most to you and look for opportunities in those areas.

✔ Talk to a career placement office.

✔ Take advantage of resources provided by related professional organizations. Associations that represent advertising, marketing, and promoting interests can help connect you to potential employers.

Interview with a Professional:
Q&A
Mark Cunningham
Vice president of promotions and marketing, Aware
Records, Chicago, Illinois

Q: *How did you get started?*

A: In college, I did several internships in the music business to prepare
for a career in this field. I interned with a concert promoter, at our university student events center in the marketing department, at a major
label distribution office, and I worked with the on-campus concert com-
mittee. I was also an Aware Rep (street team member) for Aware Records,
which helped me build the relationships that ultimately led me to this
job.

Q: *What's a typical day like?*

A: No day is ever the same in my business. I work on the marketing side
of our record label and as an artist manager. Our bands are all doing different things at different times and you constantly have to jump back and
forth from one thing to the next as the day unfolds. A big part of my job
is trying to get people to listen to or promote our bands in one way or another. Whether it's a radio station and airplay or a concert promoter advertising a show, it all revolves around more exposure and opportunity
for our artists.

Q: *What's your advice for those starting a career?*

A: Promotions and marketing are essentially sales. Whether it's trying to
get someone to like a song or pay for a concert ticket or CD, it's all about
exposing people to something you hope they'll like. My advice for starting
out is to find professionals in the field and set up an informational interview to learn about what they do and how they do it. I did that with someone in my field and he showed me in two hours what it could have taken
me two years to learn. Internships are a great starting point as well, and
they can open up all kinds of doors.

Q: *What's the best part of your job?*

A: I still feel the same way about this job as I did 10 years ago. I've always
loved hearing and seeing people react positively to the artists we work
with. There are a lot of positives about working in this business, but that
has always been the best part for me and I hope it always will be.

Career Connections

For further information, contact:

Sales and Marketing Executives International http://www.smei.org

Businessschools.com http://www.businessschools.com

Business and Professional Women's Foundation http://www .bpwusa.org

National Business Association http://www.nationalbusiness.org

Hospitality Sales and Marketing Association International http://www.hsmai.org

Associate's Degree Programs

Here are a few schools offering quality promotions programs:

Blue Ridge Community College, Flat Rock, North Carolina

Pittsburgh Technical Institute, Pittsburgh, Pennsylvania

Post University, online at http://www.post.edu

Indiana University South Bend, South Bend, Indiana

Financial Aid

Here are a few scholarships related to sales and marketing, a field of study with close ties to promotions. Tailoring your scholarship search to include business skills would also be a way of broadening your scholarship search. For more on financial aid for two-year students, please see Appendix B.

Sales and Marketing Executives International offers many scholarships through its local chapters. For example, prospective students in the Ohio area should visit http://www.smecleveland.com/Scholarship.asp.   http://www.smei.org

The **National Business Association** offers at least 10 scholarships each year for application to universities or technical schools in the United States. These one-year awards are not based on financial need. http://www.nationalbusiness.org/NBAWEB/scholarship.htm

Delta Mu Delta, a national honor society in business administration, offers students enrolled in business programs at schools where there is a chapter of Delta Mu Delta the chance to compete for related business scholarships in the society's annual awards program.   http://www .deltamudelta.org

Related Careers

Specialist in advertising, marketing, public relations, and sales; product demonstrator, market and survey researcher, writer.

Marketing Manager

Vital Statistics

Salary: Entry-level marketing jobs pay about $33,000 a year, according to the U.S. Bureau of Labor Statistics, and senior marketing managers earn a median annual salary of $63,000.

Employment: The need for marketing managers from 2004 through 2014 is expected to increase much faster than the average for all other occupations, with employment expected to expand in this job sector in the range of 18 to 26 percent, according to Bureau of Labor Statistics.

Education: An associate's degree in marketing can be completed in as little as 18 months. A solid degree will provide instruction in the principles of economics, business law, accounting, and finance. Electives in sociology, psychology, and journalism can shore up communications skills.

Work Environment: As a top managerial position, this occupation is not typically 9-to-5 in nature. Evenings, weekends, and long hours can be par for the course. The financial reward is great, and the expectations are high: According to a 2004 survey, about two-thirds in the field worked in excess of 40 hours per week.

Can you hear me now? Good. If you've ever been thoroughly entertained or at the very least held hostage by an engaging 30-second advertising spot on television, or charmed by a slogan on the side of a city bus or a billboard, you're certainly not alone. That catchy jingle on the radio, eye-popping billboard, and the possibly annoying television spot are the finished products of labs of creative marketing teams headed up by marketing managers.

What's the difference between marketing and advertising? The differences can be hard to distinguish, but basically, advertising is part of marketing. Marketing is defined as the systematic planning of activities that facilitate the exchange between a business and consumer, and it includes public relations, media planning, market research, product pricing, distribution, and customer support.

In 2004, approximately 188,000 marketing managers made their living as consumer-driven fortune tellers, anticipating the needs of the public. Their overall goal is to generate a feeling of confidence and trust in a brand or product so that a consumer is eager to buy it. The job requires launching products, then maintaining a product's image through advertising and public relations and coming up with marketing and communication plans that will maintain and expand on existing business. Some marketers are focused on developing trade with other businesses rather than the general public. Their field is called B2B or business-to-business selling.

Marketing managers handle a variety of different business tasks, from accounting to planning to hiring and firing. In the big picture, they are continuously trying to get a grasp of overall consumer spending habits so they can make sure their product will be a part of a consumer's budget. Recently, marketers have identified a consumer trend called *transumerism*. Recent research has shown that a growing portion of the population is concerned more with "experiencing" a product rather than owning it. *Transumers* are ready to pay less to rent, lease, or borrow—all in the name of having new things. For example, transumers who become members of Bag Borrow or Steal pay a monthly fee and pick and order handbags, keeping them until they're ready to trade in for a new model. Classic car clubs have seen a rise in membership as customers want to drive Ferraris, Bentleys, Lamborghinis, and a variety of other cars. Being able to identify and take advantage of trends like transumerism is a distinguishing factor for being a successful marketing manager.

In today's global economy, some marketing managers create product plans of global scope, and most have to know techniques for selling via the Internet.

> **"Now we understand that the most important thing we do is market the product. We've come around to saying that Nike is a marketing-oriented company, and the product is our most important marketing tool."**
> —Phil Knight, founder and CEO, Nike

On the Job

Marketing professionals can be found working in just about any industry—from banking to air travel to major department stores. They are the bridge builders developing a relationship between an organization or brand and its intended audience. If you think you've got a talent for anticipating consumer needs while being creative and memorable, marketing could be just the career for you.

The work combines varied business skills. The manager may be in charge of market research, product development, pricing, sales and distribution, and promotion of the product. All along the way, they are the ones who make sure staff is working according to budget and on schedule.

Marketing managers are master communicators. They spend a great deal of time writing and presenting their research to fellow workers. They pitch their marketing campaigns to their superiors and often provide updates on the effectiveness of a campaign that is in progress. They have to defend their work, showing that their plan is generating profits and operating within budget.

Typically, larger firms may provide more opportunities to rise to the level of marketing manager, and some offer their own management training programs. Some companies even provide their workers with continuing education opportunities at local learning institutions.

Keys to Success

To be a successful marketing manager, you should have:

- oral and written communication skills
- analytical abilities
- an interest in understanding consumers
- an ability to handle numbers
- a talent for leading others
- multitasking skills

Do You Have What It Takes?

Students interested in marketing should be highly motivated individuals who possess the capacity for being creative, flexible, and decisive. As cliché as it may be, an ability to communicate is vital in this field. Managers, public, and staff alike will be either turned off or sold on your ideas based on your ability to communicate persuasively.

A Typical Day at Work

As a marketing manager, your day often will depend on what stage your company is at with the development of a product or service. In the early stages, marketing managers guide the research phase. You may be reviewing initial reports by your research team about the viability of introducing a new soap into the marketplace. Your staff has compiled data on all existing soaps, including which ones are the bestsellers. Phone surveys conducted by your team indicate that a new mango-scented soap may be popular. The product development people have created a sample and you're scheduling to have random consumers test the soap in person in the near future.

After reviewing the status of this product that is just in the beginning stages, you turn your attention to a deodorant that was launched six months ago. You are currently in the middle of a big ad campaign for the deodorant, and at a conference room meeting, you and other marketers discuss how the advertising is working. You carefully look at sales versus the amount spent. You also look at where the product is selling best.

(continued on next page)

(continued from previous page)

Consumers were able to save money by clipping a coupon printed in several publications. The coupons were coded so you can review which publications were most effective in advertising your product. At the same time, you're conducting market research with consumers by phone and in person regarding this deodorant. Do users find it effective? Do they like the packaging? Which of the latest ad campaigns do they favor most?

Your work always involves looking at the big picture—understanding the roles of all those involved in your product, keeping an eye on budgets, profits, and schedules, and communicating with all staff to stay abreast of their efforts and keep them informed of the overall status of a product. You are the leader of a large team of professionals, and at the end of the day, you all have to be on the same page to make a product a hit.

How to Break In

It's almost unheard of to become a marketing manager without wearing a few hats first. Many managers cut their professional teeth starting off as purchasing agents, buyers, or sales representatives; or as product, advertising, or promotions specialists. Individuals with degrees in marketing supported by coursework in advertising, survey design, statistics, and psychology have laid a strong foundation for success in this field. An associate's degree program featuring an internship can lead to entry-level employment. Getting your foot in the door can be a function of your work experience or the portfolio you've created while at school. Participation in professional society activities can provide that networking opportunity that lands a first job interview. To advance, professionals may have to earn a higher degree or pursue further technical training. Because marketing managers can have a mastery of an entire business, some step up to become top executives. You might too— with enough experience and professional connections.

Two-Year Training

Two-year associate's degree programs in business with an emphasis in marketing develop skills specifically geared toward beginning a career. Classroom exposure to courses in business law, economics, mathematics, and accounting can make you a well-rounded job candidate. Computer literacy is especially useful in this field as database applications are vital to the operation of almost any firm, and Internet savvy has become crucial for tapping into the expanding world of e-commerce. For those looking to start in market research, coursework in statistics, math, survey design, psychology, and advertising is especially recommended.

To experience a variety of projects and clients, try getting an internship at an ad agency. If you prove yourself by helping on a few important accounts, you may be able to get started as a creative specialist. If the industry you're keen on joining is more services than goods, a stint in the trenches of sales and managing clients could connect you into the marketing department after you've wowed them with your knowledge of your company's customer base.

What to Look For in a School

The pay is rewarding and the competition is substantial in marketing. To market effectively, you must know your product or your field. Some schools have concentrations geared toward particular markets. Such concentrations include entertainment, music, sports, fashion/retail merchandising, and hotel and resort management. When considering a two-year school, be sure to ask these questions:

☞ Does your school provide an environment for developing marketing skills (i.e., business clubs, school newspaper)?

☞ Does your school provide a diverse business course curriculum that includes not only marketing but advertising or media-related communications as well?

☞ What is the school's job placement rate?

☞ Are the instructors well credentialed? Do they have the industry experience needed to be insightful?

☞ Does the school offer a concentration in your desired field?

☞ What businesses are involved in the internship program?

The Future

Competition at home and abroad in consumer products and services are engines of growth that will continue to fuel the need for skilled marketers. However, not all sectors will provide equal opportunity, according to the Bureau of Labor Statistics. Sectors including scientific, professional, and technical services are expected to grow, while a decline in manufacturing is expected. A solid academic and work background in marketing can act as a passkey into other aspects of corporate life, such as brand managers, market researchers, marketing associates, and product managers. The best opportunities will be available to those who acquire the technical skills requisite for conducting marketing on the Internet and in foreign markets.

Did You Know?

Children have become one of the fastest growing targets of marketing efforts. According to Consumeraffairs.com, the average American child today is exposed to an estimated 40,000 television commercials a year, or more than 100 a day.

Interview with a Professional: Q&A

Gianni Cortesee

E-commerce marketing manager, Limogesjewlery.com, Chicago, Illinois

Q: *How did you get started?*

A: I converted from a position in outside sales and as the company started to reorganize, I was given an opportunity to continue that path or the opportunity to go into marketing, and I chose marketing.

Q: *What's a typical day like?*

A: A typical day would involve planning, testing, analyzing, and optimizing. As a marketer you're looking at planning in a business and seasonal sense tied to certain occasions: Mother's Day, Easter; it could be something looking at new opportunities in our calendar or it could be a search engine optimization.

Q: *What's your advice for those starting a career?*

A: It's important to understand you have to pay your dues and be willing to start at the bottom. Also, you have to be very detail oriented. Part of marketing is being the face of the company; so much of marketing is making sure the right words are used. The people who lose sight of that are usually not very detail oriented, and they aren't the ones who go very far. Most of all, you have to be adaptable to your business environment, and you can't underestimate people who work hard. Be a listener.

Q: *What's the best part of your job?*

A: Coming up with positive ideas that will affect our company's bottom line and being involved in all of our marketing channels is great. I really enjoy being a decision maker, affecting the company in a positive way that can be recorded. As a result of being at a small company, I'm not locked into a pillar; it would have taken me three to four times longer to have acquired the experience and expertise were I stationed at a larger company.

Job Seeking Tips

Follow these specific tips for marketers, and then turn to Appendix A for help on creating résumés, interviewing, and collecting references.

✔ Look into resources provided by professional marketing associations.

✔ Get involved in a marketing campaign at your school—that type of experience is vital for your portfolio.

✔ Investigate opportunities with public relations and advertising firms. Communications and creative skill sets developed there can serve as a springboard to a marketing career later on.

✔ Talk to a career placement office specialist.

Career Connections

For further information, contact the following organizations.

American Marketing Association http://www.marketingpower.com

Business Marketing Association http://www.marketing.org

Talent Zoo (advertising, marketing, and public relations jobs) http://www.talentzoo.com

Associate's Degree Programs

Here are a few schools offering quality marketing programs:

The University of Toledo, Toledo, Ohio, and online

Indian River Community College, Ft. Pierce, Florida

Bauder College, Atlanta, Georgia

The College of Westchester, White Plains, New York

Financial Aid

Here are a few marketing-related scholarships. For more on financial aid for two-year students, see Appendix B.

Hospitality Sales and Marketing Association International provides students with financial assistance to pursue a career in hospitality sales and marketing.　http://www.hsmai.org/Resources/scholarships.cfm

The **American Marketing Association** extends a wide array of scholarship opportunities for marketing students and professionals. Local chapters of the association often have scholarships available, so check. For example, the Baltimore chapter provides three scholarships to contribute to the educational development of motivated students in the region.　http://www.marketingpower.com

Related Careers

Market and survey researcher, brand manager, marketing associate, marketing director, product manager.

Public
Relations
Specialist

Vital Statistics

Salary: The median annual salary for public relations specialists is $43,830, according to 2006 data from the U.S. Bureau of Labor Statistics. Those who rise to the level of public relations manager stand to make $70,000 a year.

Employment: Competition is expected to be high, but according to the Bureau of Labor Statistics, the industry is projected to grow 22 percent over the 2004–2014 period, substantially faster than the average for all jobs.

Education: An associate's degree in public relations can be completed in as little as two years. A strong associate's degree program will provide instruction in communications, advertising, and marketing along with liberal arts courses.

Work Environment: PR experts ply their trade in comfortable offices, sitting at desks equipped with computers. As deadlines approach, these professionals put in long hours, often extending into evenings and weekends.

Persuasion can move mountains. The six-pack of A&W Root Beer in your bag of groceries, the Levi's jeans you're wearing, and your decision to cast a vote for Proposition X or Candidate Y are all outcomes of opinions formed in large part by marketing, advertising, and public relations.

Public relations efforts are often part of an entire marketing plan that will also include advertising. These specialists do exactly what their name implies. They maintain relations with the public on behalf of businesses, nonprofit associations, universities, hospitals, and other organizations.

Public relations professionals fight to get media attention for their clients, whether it's 15 seconds on the radio or 15 inches of story in the newspaper. Where advertising managers buy space or airtime to tout a product, public relations managers look to get free attention from the media by finding the news angle about their clients. They often write press releases that explain why their client is newsworthy and then spread the word to television, radio, magazines, and newspapers.

Press releases can announce a new-flavored cola aimed at teenagers, the appointment of a new college dean, or the expansion of a fast-food chain. PR specialists often have to target these releases to very specific media. The *CBS Evening News* may not care about a new maple-flavored cola, but *Beverage Digest* will, and so might the Food Network.

Public relations pros focus on building, managing, and sustaining a positive public image. They always look for the angle or "spin" they can put on news regarding their client. Sometimes, negative things happen to a client, and it's the PR pro's job to put as much positive "spin" on events as possible. They are on the front lines when the press needs answers about a client's actions. For example, when Exxon had the Valdez oil spill in 1989, the PR staff fielded questions and explained how Exxon would take care of the accident. They had to try and put the best face on the situation. If the client is a rock star who smashed up a hotel room, the star's PR agent may face the press and explain that the star had been under enormous stress as of late.

Although PR and advertising agencies can be found nationwide, most are located in major media markets. New York and California combined account for a quarter of all workers in the industry and one in five established firms. Although a lot of work in this field can be found in big cities, most PR managers work for small firms. A whopping 68 percent of advertising and PR firms employ five people or fewer, and the Bureau of Labor Statistics counted 61,000 self-employed workers within the industry in 2004.

On the Job

Public relations managers direct publicity programs to a targeted audience. Whether their cause is a line of products, an environmental group, or a political candidate, their ultimate goal is to get media exposure.

To achieve that, PR folks use all their communication skills. They call writers and producers in to pitch ideas. They write press releases that are crafted as news stories that may be picked up by the media. PR representatives also know how to turn on a smile, shake hands, and work a crowd during social events with the media and public.

Those higher up in an organization direct staff, overseeing their writing efforts and media calls. Beginners in the field frequently start out as research or account assistants before they move up to positions as account executives or supervisors. Sometimes PR people arrange speaking engagements for their clients, write the speeches, and assemble presentations for community forums or corporate affairs. A PR writer may be in charge of creating a Microsoft Office Suite PowerPoint presentation explaining an energy company's latest improvements regarding air quality and waste disposal. They may also be responsible for preparing annual reports and writing proposals for various projects.

Managers have to meet with other executives in a firm to discuss their efforts and make sure that the overall PR program is in step with the organization's goals. Often, they meet with other members of the marketing team to review how PR corresponds with advertising plans.

Keys to Success

To be successful in public relations, you need:
- strong organizational skills
- the ability to think far in advance
- oral and written communication skills
- an appetite for media and an eye for new markets
- a flair for creativity
- comfort addressing the public
- the power of persuasion

Do You Have What It Takes?

Students who wish to pursue a career in public relations should have strong organizational skills, a penchant for communication, and the ability to master an area of expertise. After all, it will be your job to represent your client or your product in a confident, no-doubt-about-it manner. Aspiring professionals in this field should be social chameleons at some level, possessing the ability to connect with a wide variety of audiences. Thicker-than-average skin may be necessary for dealing with editors who can be the porcupines of the 9-to-5 world when you catch them on the wrong side of a deadline. Those who have experience with public speaking or debate, writing for the school newspaper, or working on a local or student government campaign often have some of the skills necessary to thrive in this career.

A Typical Day at Work

Whether working for a political candidate, nonprofit, or business, public relations managers spend large parts of their day developing press releases and phoning magazine and newspaper editors. Working from a database of telephone numbers, e-mail, and fax numbers (yes, newsrooms still have fax machines), PR firms create avalanches of press releases designed to come across as news. Although most news organizations start off with a morning battle plan for what they're going to cover, these media have space or airtime to fill. Indeed, a great number of reports, articles, and stories can be traced back to the desk of a public relations professional.

While most of their tasks are completed without leaving their desks, PR experts often have to get out there and schmooze both public and media at community meetings, press functions, and other events. They also spend a portion of their day coordinating with the rest of their PR team, making sure their activities are aligning with the overall goal of a PR and marketing program.

How to Break In

While cracking the books at school, young public relations professionals must put in a dedicated effort to develop a portfolio that will show your range of talents and illustrate your drive and ambition to future employers. Typically, PR firms have a habit of gravitating toward individuals who are experts in one field or another. However, the field of public relations is particularly peppered with internship possibilities. Some larger PR firms have formal training programs. If you have a particular field in mind (i.e., health care, finance, Save the Lemurs, etc.), gain as much knowledge as possible about the industry and issues before setting foot in the door. In PR, it will be your job to grab an editor's attention, so in addition to developing a knowledge base, take whatever opportunity you can to demonstrate your wordsmith abilities. A college newspaper can be a good place to start. In high school, take courses in communications, English, and media studies. Learning a foreign language may open work options on international accounts. Fluency in Spanish may prove quite useful in markets such as Miami, Houston, and Los Angeles, where an ever-larger Hispanic community is becoming a targeted and prized audience as the number of Spanish-language television, radio, and print outlets grows.

Two-Year Training

Many community colleges offer two-year associate's degree programs in public relations. While coursework may focus on writing press releases, mass media communications and public speech students may also take classes in journalism, advertising, psychology, and English. Other courses may include public relations principles and techniques; public relations management and administration; and writing proposals, annual reports, scripts, speeches, and related items. Some classes may cover visual communications, with a focus on desktop publishing and computer graphics; and research, highlighting social science research and survey design and implementation. Students are advised to develop an expertise—whether it be in technology, health, science, engineering, sales, or finance, for example. Real-world experience often counts more than grades, so make sure your two-year training includes an internship or part-time work in the field.

What to Look For in a School

When considering a two-year school, be certain to ask these questions:

☞ Is the school located in a market with an ample supply of media outlets?

☞ What is the school's job placement rate?

☞ Where are current graduates working now?

☞ Does the school have the connections necessary for providing a meaningful internship?

☞ Does the school offer related coursework, such as media studies and journalism?

☞ Do your teachers possess industry experience?

The Future

New jobs will be created as the economy expands and generates more products and services to advertise. Increased demand for public relations services will also stem from growth in the number and types of media outlets used to reach consumers, including the Internet, cable television, and satellite radio.

Did You Know?

In a great PR coup, all three major U.S. television networks (Fox didn't exist back then) carried the opening ceremonies of McDonald's first Moscow restaurant in 1990.

Job Seeking Tips

According to the Bureau of Labor Statistics, administrative support jobs accounted for 28 percent of all advertising and PR positions in 2004. If you're having a hard time landing an ideal entry-level job, consider becoming a known quantity by accepting an internship or part-time work. Then try to trade up as openings present themselves.

✔ Seek advice from your career placement office.

✔ Join student groups related to public relations. For details, look into the Public Relations Student Society of America (http://www.prssa.org).

✔ Develop an online résumé and portfolio. The portfolio may include a mock public relations campaign that you developed on your own.

✔ Pursue a position in an industry that interests you and try to develop as much expertise in that area as possible.

✔ Increase your credentials and marketability through certification. The International Association of Business Communicators (http://www.iabc.com) accredits public relations specialists, as does the Universal Accreditation Board, which accredits public relations specialists who are members of the Public Relations Society of America (http://www.prsa.org).

Interview with a Professional:
Q&A
Larn Stache

Public relations marketing manager, MBM Company
(manufacturer of costume and precious decorative
jewelry), Chicago, Illinois

Q: *How did you get started?*

A: I was doing marketing for MBM Company, and it occurred to me they
were not doing any kind of public relations and our products weren't getting a lot of editorial placement. So, I asked our president if I could start
our PR department and he said yes. Now I try to get our products in magazines and other publications for free.

Q: *What's a typical day like?*

A: I spend a lot of time writing editors to inquire about what kind of content they're looking for and to see what kind of samples they are looking
for. Editors probably get 100 e-mails a day, and it's your job to stay on their
minds. If a competitor's product gets into a magazine it looks bad, and we
don't want fashion consumers to think of anyone but us, that's part of my
day. Oftentimes I spend the other part of my day attending to editors when
they do want something; I have to request something from the warehouse
and then package it in such a way that it stands out to the editor—that's important because we know ours won't be the only product an editor sees.

Q: *What's your advice for those starting a career?*

A: Any kind of retail company, whether online or brick-and-mortar, should
have somebody who is responsible for contacting newspaper and magazine
editors. Every business should be doing PR, even if you don't go in as a PR
specialist. If you're starting out and your company doesn't have a public relations department per se, see if you can approach them with a campaign.
Part of the reason they let me do this is because I was doing e-mail customer
relations and I was familiar with our line of products. Obviously, if your job
is so busy you don't have time to take in PR, you shouldn't ask for it. However, if you have time and you feel like you need a new challenge, it's a great
place to be.

Q: *What's the best part of your job?*

A: It's very exciting to see your company's products in a magazine; it's
proof to see what you've done actually works. Magazines are typically what
tell consumers what fashions are going to be in style. Most magazines have
a two- or three-month lead time, and in July I'm already finding out what's
going to be in style this fall, so it's interesting to plan ahead.

Career Connections

For further information, contact:

> **Public Relations Student Society of America** http://www.prssa.org/
>
> **The International Association of Business Communicator** http://www.iabc.com
>
> **Council of Public Relations Firms** http://www.prfirms.org/
>
> **WorkinPR** http://www.workinpr.com

> ## "The only thing worse than being talked about is not to be talked about at all."
> ### —Oscar Wilde, playwright

Associate's Degree Programs

Here are a few schools offering quality public relations and advertising programs:

> *Ellis College of New York Institute of Technology,* online at http://ellis.nyit.edu/
>
> *Xavier University,* Cincinnati, Ohio
>
> *College of Business Technology,* Kendall, Florida
>
> *University College of Tulane,* New Orleans, Louisiana
>
> *Parkland College,* Champaign, Illinois

Financial Aid

Various chapters of the **Public Relations Society of America and the Public Relations Student Society of America** offer scholarships in the spring to college students who are members of the Public Relations Society of America. Check the Web site as listed above in Career Connections to find the chapter closest to you. Although the above-mentioned organizations would likely be the best place to start, you can also check out the scholarship below. For more information on financial aid for two-year students, turn to Appendix B.

The **Foundation of Women Executives in Public Relations** has awards for both men and women majoring in public relations. http://www.wepr.org

Related Careers

Account manager, assistant account manager, creative director, copy chief, art director, media director, copywriter, art director, graphic designer, research executive, market research analyst, media planner, media buyer, advertising sales agent, product demonstrator, and product promoter.

Insurance Agent

Vital Statistics

Salary: The median annual income for insurance agents is $41,720, according to 2006 data from the U.S. Bureau of Labor Statistics.

Employment: Overall employment of insurance agents is expected to grow less quickly than for other fields, but as the population expands and many reach retirement age, demand for products in the area of auto insurance, health insurance, and home owner's insurance will continue to rise. According to a 2006 survey by the National Association of Colleges and Employers, jobs with insurance companies appear to be one of the "best bets" for two-year graduates.

Education: Candidates with proven sales ability may be hired out of high school and those who spend the state-required hours preparing for and passing the state-license test may sell insurance within a year. However, in more competitive job markets and for more involved aspects of the industry, a college background with coursework in banking and financial support services or other insurance aspects will provide a leg up when applying for jobs or seeking career advancement. Prerequisites: finance, mathematics, accounting, marketing, economics, business administration.

Work Environment: With a small office typically serving as home base, insurance agents spend a considerable amount of time traveling a local radius, meeting with clients to close sales or investigate claims, occasionally scheduling evening and weekend appointments to suit their clients' scheduling needs. Most work in or near major cities, and although some are employed at large headquarters, most employees operate out of local offices or independent agencies.

Whether they are offering a "piece of the rock," the advice of "a good neighbor," or the imagery of a confident, galloping stag, insurance companies, including Prudential, State Farm, and Hartford Financial, are in the business of selling peace of mind. Insurance agents provide financial protection when the unexpected happens. If you are insured and have a car accident, medical emergency, or even a loss of life, insurance policies pay money to help families meet sudden expenses. In return for this financial protection, policyholders pay monthly, quarterly, or annual premiums.

Typically, insurance agents offer products designed to insulate policyholders from a worst-case scenario that could wreak havoc on physical property and well-being alike. Property and auto insurance carriers pay for repairs if the fire department doesn't get there in time to save your house or if someone sideswipes your car. Policies can also protect against natural disasters, such as hurricanes, earthquakes, and tornadoes. Health and life insurance providers pay for treatment for those who get sick or provide funding to a family should a family member unexpectedly die. Today's insurance providers often sell other financial services as well, such as estate planning, money management, and retirement plans.

Employment of insurance agents is expected to rise up to 8 percent between 2004 and 2014, according to the Bureau of Labor Statistics. Currently about 400,000 individuals work in this industry. Of the more than 1,800 companies in the field, the top 20 players typically generate more than $800 billion in revenue per year. Demand is considerably greater for college graduates with a variety of insurance and financial abilities. If you can pick up a second language, your marketability goes up even further.

On the Job

More than anything else, insurance agents have the ability to relate to people. They often sit down face to face with clients and find out about their lives. If the client has three kids, a car, and a new home, the insurance agent knows that this person will need money if an accident strikes his or her family, home, or possessions. Good agents know how to interact with customers from a variety of backgrounds, and the more they can get to know about a potential client's life, the better they can assess a customer's financial concerns.

Agents also need to delve into personal lives to gauge how big a risk the customer may be. If a life insurance agent discovers that you are a regular sky diver who smokes five packs of cigarettes a day, your life insurance premium is going to be sky high (no pun intended) because you're at a much greater risk of dying than a nonsmoker who doesn't jump out of planes.

Beyond people skills, good communication, marketing, and organizational abilities are important to being an insurance agent. They also need to have a knack for numbers in order to add up a person's finances and calculate how much protection the individual needs.

Agents manage stacks of paperwork as clients must sign detailed contracts explaining the terms of their protection. As with most sales jobs, insurance agents hustle because their wages rise as they earn more sales commissions. Agents are always looking for leads and potential new business. This can mean working the phones, calling people to discuss their current insurance coverage and explaining how their company's coverage may be better. To meet more potential clients, agents are often active in their community, participating in Rotary, Elks, or other local volunteer groups.

Keys to Success

To be a successful insurance agent you need:

- ➤ the ability to connect with people from a variety of backgrounds
- ➤ strong analytical skills for evaluating a client's needs
- ➤ good written and communications skills
- ➤ good oral and writing skills
- ➤ the ability to inspire confidence in your customers

Do You Have What It Takes?

To be a good insurance agent, you should have a genuine interest in helping others. That concern for helping people achieve the right level of financial protection directly translates into more sales and increasing commissions. You also need to be a strong communicator, especially as a speaker since most of your sales will be based on how you orally pitch potential clients about how your services can meet their needs. Keeping track of current customers and prospects takes organization—from filing contracts to scheduling meetings to reviewing policies. You have to be able to handle a calendar filled with in-home appointments, phone calls, office work, and social engagements.

A Typical Day at Work

As an insurance agent, you may start work at 9 in the morning and end by 5 p.m. some days, but you also have to put in hours at night and on weekends when customers have time to discuss their personal affairs. Your schedule may accommodate a prospective client who comes in off the street, fielding phone calls asking for rate quotes, a luncheon honoring community volunteers, and a meeting at 7 o'clock that night with a new father who wants life insurance to financially protect his wife and son. You rely on your phone skills for a large part of the day. Your ability to extract details from a diverse cross-section of people and match them with your company's policy offerings is how you earn your keep. When you can pull your ear away from the phone, you take time to think about your marketing efforts and make plans to distribute fliers for your services in mailboxes and take out an ad in the local paper and on local buses. You also take a look at your Web site and make notes on how you can make it more attractive to potential clients.

How to Break In

One of the best ways to become an insurance agent is to work as an assistant under a seasoned professional while you study for the state-licensing exam or take your associate's degree courses, or both! If you are enrolled in a sales, business, or insurance program at a local community college or university, your school should have some established connections that will help you find an internship with a company. Companies love interns and your prospects for passing the state exam and taking on more responsibility increase with the amount of real-world experience you've had in the field.

> **"You don't need to pray to God any more when there are storms in the sky, but you do have to be insured."**
> —**Bertolt Brecht**

Two-Year Training

Two-year associate's degrees in business with an emphasis on specific insurance training will lay the groundwork needed to attain an entry-level job in the field. An insurance curriculum covers such material as estate planning, asset allocation, annuities, and regulatory information that is targeted to this industry and financial services. More general courses cover business administration, business law, math, marketing, economics, finance, and accounting. Prospective insurance agents looking to improve or develop their sales techniques may profit greatly from coursework in public speaking, psychology, and sociology. It also pays to get some training in the software packages that have become industry standard in this field.

Similar to real estate agents, insurance sales agents must obtain a license in the state or states where they plan to do their selling. Separate licenses are required for agents to sell life and health insurance and property and casualty insurance. In most states, licenses are issued only to applicants who complete specified courses and who pass state examinations covering insurance fundamentals and the state's insurance laws.

To advance, a number of organizations offer professional designation programs that certify one's expertise in specialties such as life, health, and property and casualty insurance, as well as financial consulting. Another option for enhancing a career is to become a certified financial planner by completing a set of educational requirements and passing a comprehensive exam. Check with the Certified Financial Planner Board of Standards (http://www.cfp.net).

What to Look For in a School

When considering a two-year school, be certain to ask these questions:

☞ What is the school's job placement rate?

☞ What is the success rate of graduates for passing the state-licensing exam?

☞ What are the credentials of your potential instructors? Have they worked in the industry?

☞ Does the school offer the courses you'll need to develop the skills to market yourself?

The Future

In a world in which customer service can mean getting lost in a maze of automated phone choices, there is still a need for real humans to discuss insurance needs with clients. According to the Bureau of Labor Statistics, sales of health insurance and long-term-care insurance are expected to rise sharply as the population ages. Also, a swelling population will heighten the demand for insurance for automobiles, homes, and high-priced valuables and equipment. As new businesses emerge and existing firms expand their insurance coverage, sales of commercial insurance are also expected to increase. Such commercial coverage may include product liability, workers' compensation, employee benefits, and pollution liability insurance.

Job Seeking Tips

Follow these specific tips, and then turn to Appendix A for help on creating résumés, interviewing, and collecting references.

✔ If you live in a border area, consider preparing for and passing tests in multiple states.

✔ Pick up a foreign language if you can. Fluency in Spanish or another language could be what separates you from the rest in building your customer base.

✔ Talk to insurance companies during your schooling to learn which branch or specialty of insurance suits you best.

✔ Talk to the career placement office.

✔ Join any helpful student groups such as a business students association.

Interview with a Professional:
Q&A

Gloria M. Bruno

Risk management consultant, president of the
National Association of Insurance Women International,
Tulsa, Oklahoma

Q: *How did you get started?*

A: My mother was a marine underwriter for a large national company. I worked in her office during the summers and as needed. It was a natural progression to go into the same industry full time, after I graduated and married.

Q: *What's a typical day like?*

A: My days are not really typical. I "retired" from retail insurance sales in 2000 and now provide risk management consulting services to a variety of clientele ranging from local municipalities to hospital districts to the airport to larger retail or wholesale risks. My day could consist of visiting with these clients, their CPAs, or attorneys. Or I could be sitting at the desk researching, reading through policies or contracts on their behalf, or driving to Baton Rouge to deal with some state political entity on their behalf.

Q: *What's your advice for those starting a career?*

A: Get a degree, learn all you can about current technology, and then decide which of the many, many facets of this vast industry appeal to you and fit your personality. It is really difficult to get up in the morning and go to a job you dislike. Make sure you enjoy what you do. Your feelings show through. This is a person-to-person industry. The client will know if you are not happy. Never stop learning. Never become complacent.

Q: *What's the best part of your job?*

A: The interaction with people! The satisfaction of knowing you are a problem-solver and that you helped someone save or replace their assets. . . . There are lots of "best parts."

Did You Know?

Some celebrities insure parts of their body because that's what earns them money. Keith Richards, guitarist of the Rolling Stones, insured his hands, and Dolly Parton insured her breasts. The iconic actress and singer Marlene Dietrich insured her voice for $1 million (http://www.bankrate.com).

Career Connections

For further information, contact:

Insurance Information Institute http://www.iii.org

Risk and Insurance Management Society http://www.rims.org

Property and Casualty.com http://www.propertyandcasualty.com

National Association of Insurance Women http://www.naiw.org

Associate's Degree Programs

Here are a few schools offering quality insurance education programs:

Jefferson State Community College, Birmingham, Alabama

Saint Louis Community College, St. Louis, Missouri

Community College of Southern Nevada, North Las Vegas, Nevada

Hagerstown Community College, Hagerstown, Maryland

City College of San Francisco, San Francisco, California

Financial Aid

See below for an insurance-related scholarship. For more on financial aid for two-year students, please see Appendix B.

The **National Association of Professional Surplus Lines Offices Insurance Scholarship Program** offers scholarships to "deserving college and university students majoring in insurance." http://www .napslo.org

Related Careers

Financial analyst, financial manager, personal financial advisor, insurance underwriter, claims adjuster, claims examiner, claims investigator; securities, commodities, and financial service sales agent.

Appendix A
Tools for Career Success

When 20-year-old Justin Schulman started job-hunting for a position as a fitness trainer—his first step toward managing a fitness facility—he didn't mess around. "I immediately opened the Yellow Pages and started calling every number listed under health and fitness, inquiring about available positions," he recalls. Schulman's energy and enterprise paid off: He wound up with interviews that led to several offers of part-time work.

Schulman's experience highlights an essential lesson for jobseekers: There are plenty of opportunities out there, but jobs won't come to you—especially the career-oriented, well-paying ones that that you'll want to stick with over time. You've got to seek them out.

Uncover Your Interests

Whether you're in high school or bringing home a full-time paycheck, the first step toward landing your ideal job is assessing your interests. You need to figure out what makes you tick. After all, there is a far greater chance that you'll enjoy and succeed in a career that taps into your passions, inclinations, and natural abilities. That's what happened with career-changer Scott Rolfe. He was already 26 when he realized he no longer wanted to work in the food industry. "I'm an avid outdoorsman," Rolfe says, "and I have an appreciation for natural resources that many people take for granted." Rolfe turned his passions into his ideal job as a forest technician.

If you have a general idea of what your interests are, you're far ahead of the game. You may know that you're cut out for a health care career, for instance, or one in business. You can use a specific volume of *Top Careers in Two Years* to discover what position to target. If you are unsure of your direction, check out the whole range of volumes to see the scope of jobs available. Ask yourself, what job or jobs would I most like to do if I *already* had the training and skills? Then remind yourself that this is what your two-year training will accomplish.

You can also use interest inventories and skills-assessment programs to further pinpoint your ideal career. Your school or public librarian or guidance counselor should be able to help you locate such assessments. Web sites such as America's Career InfoNet (http://www.acinet.org) and JobWeb (http://www.jobweb.com) also offer interest inventories. Don't forget the help advisers at any two-year college can provide to target your interests. You'll find suggestions for Web sites related to specific careers at the end of each chapter in any *Top Careers in Two Years* volume.

Unlock Your Network

The next stop toward landing the perfect job is networking. The word may make you cringe. But networking isn't about putting on a suit, walking into a roomful of strangers, and pressing your business card on everyone. Networking is simply introducing yourself and exchanging job-related and other information that may prove helpful to one or both of you. That's what Susan Tinker-Muller did. Quite a few years ago, she struck up a conversation with a fellow passenger on her commuter train. Little did she know that the natural interest she expressed in the woman's accounts payable department would lead to news about a job opening there. Tinker-Muller's networking landed her an entry-level position in accounts payable with MTV Networks. She is now the accounts payable administrator.

Tinker-Muller's experience illustrates why networking is so important. Fully 80 percent of openings are *never* advertised, and more than half of all employees land their jobs through networking, according to the U.S. Bureau of Labor Statistics. That's 8 out of 10 jobs that you'll miss if you don't get out there and talk with people. And don't think you can bypass face-to-face conversations by posting your résumé on job sites like Monster.com and Hotjobs.com and then waiting for employers to contact you. That's so mid-1990s! Back then, tens of thousands, if not millions, of job seekers diligently posted their résumés on scores of sites. Then they sat back and waited . . . and waited . . . and waited. You get the idea. Big job sites like Monster and Hotjobs have their place, of course, but relying solely on an Internet job search is about as effective as throwing your résumé into a black hole.

Begin your networking efforts by making a list of people to talk to: teachers, classmates (and their parents), anyone you've worked with, neighbors, worship acquaintances, and anyone you've interned or volunteered with. You can also expand your networking opportunities through the student sections of industry associations (listed at the end of each chapter of *Top Careers in Two Years*); attending or volunteering at industry events, association conferences, career fairs; and through job-shadowing. Keep in mind that only rarely will any of the people on your list be in a position to offer you a job. But whether they know it or not, they probably know someone who knows someone who is. That's why your networking goal is not to ask for a job but the name of someone to talk with. Even when you network with an employer, it's wise to say something like, "You may not have any positions available, but might you know someone I could talk with to find out more about what it's like to work in this field?"

Also, keep in mind that networking is a two-way street. For instance, you may be talking with someone who has a job opening that isn't appropriate for you. If you can refer someone else to the employer, either person may well be disposed to help you someday in the future.

Dial-Up Help

Call your contacts directly, rather than e-mail them. (E-mails are too easy for busy people to ignore, even if they don't mean to.) Explain that you're a recent graduate in your field; that Mr. Jones referred you; and that you're wondering if you could stop by for 10 or 15 minutes at your contact's convenience to find out a little more about how the industry works. If you leave this message as a voicemail, note that you'll call back in a few days to follow up. If you reach your contact directly, expect that they'll say they're too busy at the moment to see you. Ask, "Would you mind if I check back in a couple of weeks?" Then jot down a note in your date book or set up a reminder in your computer calendar and call back when it's time. (Repeat this above scenario as needed, until you get a meeting.)

Once you have arranged to talk with someone in person, prep yourself. Scour industry publications for insightful articles; having up-to-date knowledge about industry trends shows your networking contacts that you're dedicated and focused. Then pull together questions about specific employers and suggestions that will set you apart from the job-hunting pack in your field. The more specific your questions (for instance, about one type of certification versus another), the more likely your contact will see you as an "insider," worthy of passing along to a potential employer. At the end of any networking meeting, ask for the name of someone else who might be able to help you further target your search.

Get a Lift

When you meet with a contact in person (as well as when you run into someone fleetingly), you need an "elevator speech." This is a summary of up to two minutes that introduces who you are, as well as your experience and goals. An elevator speech should be short enough to be delivered during an elevator ride with a potential employer from the ground level to a high floor. In it, it's helpful to show that 1) you know the business involved; 2) you know the company; 3) you're qualified (give your work and educational information); and 4) you're goal-oriented, dependable, and hardworking. You'll be surprised how much information you can include in two minutes. Practice this speech in front of a mirror until you have the key points down very well. It should sound natural though, and you should come across as friendly, confident, and assertive. Remember, good eye contact needs to be part of your presentation as well as your everyday approach when meeting prospective employers or leads.

Get Your Résumé Ready

In addition to your elevator speech, another essential job-hunting tool is your résumé. Basically, a résumé is a little snapshot of you in words, reduced to one 8½ x 11-inch sheet of paper (or, at most, two sheets). You need a résumé whether you're in high school, college, or the workforce, and whether you've never held a job or have had many.

At the top of your résumé should be your heading. This is your name, address, phone numbers, and your e-mail address, which can be a sticking point. E-mail addresses such as sillygirl@yahoo.com or drinkingbuddy @hotmail.com won't score you any points. In fact they're a turn-off. So if you dreamed up your address after a night on the town, maybe it's time to upgrade. (Similarly, these days potential employers often check Myspace sites, personal blogs, and Web pages. What's posted there has been known to cost candidates a job offer.)

The first section of your résumé is a concise Job Objective (e.g., "Entry-level agribusiness sales representative seeking a position with a leading dairy cooperative"). These days, with word-processing software, it's easy and smart to adapt your job objective to the position for which you're applying. An alternative way to start a résumé, which some recruiters prefer, is to re-work the Job Objective into a Professional Summary. A Professional Summary doesn't mention the position you're seeking, but instead focuses on your job strengths (e.g., "Entry-level agribusiness sales rep; strengths include background in feed, fertilizer, and related markets and ability to contribute as a member of a sales team"). Which is better? It's your call.

The body of a résumé typically starts with your Job Experience. This is a chronological list of the positions you've held (particularly the ones that will help you land the job you want). Remember: never, never any fudging. However, it is okay to include volunteer positions and internships on the chronological list, as long as they're noted for what they are.

Next comes your Education section. Note: It's acceptable to flip the order of your Education and Job Experience sections if you're still in high school or have gone straight to college and don't have significant work experience. Summarize the major courses in your degree area, any certifications you've achieved, relevant computer knowledge, special seminars, or other school-related experience that will distinguish you. Include your grade average if it's more than 3.0. Don't worry if you haven't finished your degree. Simply write that you're currently enrolled in your program (if you are).

In addition to these elements, other sections may include professional organizations you belong to and any work-related achievements, awards, or recognition you've received. Also, you can have a section for your interests, such as playing piano or soccer (and include any notable achievements regarding your interests, for instance, placed third in Midwest Regional Piano Competition). You should also note other special abilities, such as "Fluent in French" or "Designed own Web site." These sorts of activities will reflect well on you, whether or not they are job-related.

You can either include your references or simply note, "References upon Request." Be sure to ask your references for permission to use their names and alert them to the fact that they may be contacted, before you include them on your résumé. For more information on résumé writing, check out Web sites such as http://www.resume.monster.com.

Craft Your Cover Letter

When you apply for a job either online or by mail, it's appropriate to include a cover letter. A cover letter lets you convey extra information about yourself that doesn't fit or isn't always appropriate in your résumé. For instance, in a cover letter, you can and should mention the name of anyone who referred you to the job. You can go into some detail about the reason you're a great match, given the job description. You also can address any questions that might be raised in the potential employer's mind (for instance, a gap in your résumé). Don't, however, ramble on. Your cover letter should stay focused on your goal: to offer a strong, positive impression of yourself and persuade the hiring manager that you're worth an interview. Your cover letter gives you a chance to stand out from the other applicants and sell yourself. In fact, 23 percent of hiring managers say a candidate's ability to relate his or her experience to the job at hand is a top hiring consideration, according to a Careerbuilder.com survey.

You can write a positive, yet concise cover letter in three paragraphs: An introduction containing the specifics of the job you're applying for; a summary of why you're a good fit for the position and what you can do for the company; and a closing with a request for an interview, contact information, and thanks. Remember to vary the structure and tone of your cover letter. For instance, don't begin every sentence with "I."

Ace Your Interview

Preparation is the key to acing any job interview. This starts with researching the company or organization you're interviewing with. Start with the firm, group, or agency's own Web site. Explore it thoroughly; read about their products and services, their history, and sales and marketing information.

Check out their news releases, links that they provide, and read up on or Google members of the management team to get an idea of what they may be looking for in their employees.

Sites such as http://www.hoovers.com enable you to research companies across many industries. Trade publications in any industry (such as *Food Industry News, Hotel Business,* and *Hospitality Technology*) are also available online or in hard copy at many college or public libraries. Don't forget to make a phone call to contacts you have in the organization to get an even better idea of the company culture.

Preparation goes beyond research, however. It includes practicing answers to common interview questions:

- ☞ *Tell me about yourself* (Don't talk about your favorite bands or your personal history; give a brief summary of your background and interest in the particular job area.)
- ☞ *Why do you want to work here?* (Here's where your research into the company comes into play; talk about the firm's strengths and products or services.)
- ☞ *Why should we hire you?* (Now is your chance to sell yourself as a dependable, trustworthy, effective employee.)
- ☞ *Why did you leave your last job?* (This is not a talk show. Keep your answer short; never bad-mouth a previous employer. You can always simply say something such as, "It wasn't a good fit, and I was ready for other opportunities.")

Rehearse your answers, but don't try to memorize them. Responses that are natural and spontaneous come across better. Trying to memorize exactly what you want to say is likely to both trip you up and make you sound robotic.

As for the actual interview, to break the ice, offer a few pleasant remarks about the day, a photo in the interviewer's office, or something else similar. Then, once the interview gets going, listen closely and answer the questions you're asked, versus making any other point that you want to convey. If you're unsure whether your answer was adequate, simply ask, "Did that answer the question?" Show respect, good energy, and enthusiasm, and be upbeat. Employers are looking for people who are enjoyable to be around, as well as good workers. Show that you have a positive attitude and can get along well with others by not bragging during the interview, overstating your experience, or giving the appearance of being too self-absorbed. Avoid one-word answers, but at the same time don't blather. If you're faced with a silence after giving your response, pause for a few seconds, and then ask, "Is there anything else you'd like me to add?" Never look at your watch or answer your cellphone during an interview.

Near the interview's end, the interviewer is likely to ask you if you have any questions. Make sure that you have a few prepared, for instance:

☞ *"Tell me about the production process."*

☞ *"What's your biggest short-term challenge?"*

☞ *"How have recent business trends affected the company?"*

☞ *"Is there anything else that I can provide you with to help you make your decision?"*

☞ *"When will you make your hiring decision?"*

During a first interview, never ask questions like, "What's the pay?" "What are the benefits?" or "How much vacation time will I get?"

Find the Right Look

Appropriate dressing and grooming is also essential to interviewing success. For business jobs and many other occupations, it's appropriate to come to an interview in a nice (not stuffy) suit. However, different fields have various dress codes. In the music business, for instance, "business casual" reigns for many jobs. This is a slightly modified look, where slacks and a jacket are just fine for a guy, and a nice skirt and blouse and jacket or sweater are acceptable for a woman. Dressing overly "cool" will usually backfire.

In general, watch all of the basics from the shoes on up (no sneakers or sandals, and no overly high heels or short skirts for women). Also avoid attention-getting necklines, girls. Keep jewelry and other "bling" to a minimum. Tattoos and body jewelry are becoming more acceptable, but if you can take out piercings (other than in your ear), you're better off. Similarly, unusual hairstyles or colors may bias an employer against you, rightly or wrongly. Make sure your hair is neat and acceptable (get a haircut?). Also go light on the makeup, self-tanning products, body scents, and other grooming agents. Don't wear a baseball cap or any other type of hat; and by all means, take off your sunglasses!

Beyond your physical appearance, you already know to be well bathed to minimize odor (leave your home early if you tend to sweat, so you can cool off in private), make good eye contact, smile, speak clearly using proper English, use good posture (don't slouch), offer a firm handshake, and arrive within five minutes of your interview. (If you're unsure of where you're going, "Mapquest" it and consider making a dry-run to the site so you won't be late.) First impressions can make or break your interview.

Remember Follow-Up

After your interview, send a thank you note. This thoughtful gesture will separate you from most of the other candidates. It demonstrates your ability to follow through, and it catches your prospective employer's attention one more time. In a 2005 Careerbuilder.com survey, nearly 15 percent of 650 hiring managers said they wouldn't hire someone who failed to send a thank you letter after the interview. Thirty-two percent say they would still consider the candidate, but would think less of him or her.

So do you hand write or e-mail the thank you letter? The fact is that format preferences vary. One in four hiring managers prefer to receive a thank you note in e-mail form only; 19 percent want the e-mail, followed up with a hard copy; 21 percent want a typed hard-copy only; and 23 percent prefer just a handwritten note. (Try to check with an assistant on the format your potential employer prefers.) Otherwise, sending an e-mail and a handwritten copy is a safe way to proceed.

Winning an Offer

There are no sweeter words to a job hunter than, "We'd like to hire you." So naturally, when you hear them, you may be tempted to jump at the offer. *Don't.* Once an employer wants you, he or she will usually give you some time to make your decision and get any questions you may have answered. Now is the time to get specific about salary and benefits, and negotiate some of these points. If you haven't already done so, check out salary ranges for your position and area of the country on sites such as Payscale.com, Salary.com, and Salaryexpert.com (basic info is free; specific requests are not). Also, find out what sorts of benefits similar jobs offer. Then don't be afraid to negotiate in a diplomatic way. Asking for better terms is reasonable and expected. You may worry that asking the employer to bump up his offer may jeopardize your job, but handled intelligently, negotiating for yourself in fact may be a way to impress your future employer—and get a better deal for yourself.

After you've done all the hard work that successful job-hunting requires, you may be tempted to put your initiative into autodrive. However, the efforts you made to land your job-from clear communication to enthusiasm-are necessary now to pave your way to continued success. As Danielle Little, a human-resources assistant, says, "You must be enthusiastic and take the initiative. There is an urgency to prove yourself and show that you are capable of performing any and all related tasks. If your manager notices that you have potential, you will be given additional responsibilities, which will help advance your career." So do your best work on the job, and build your credibility. Your payoff will be career advancement and increased earnings.

Appendix B

Financial Aid

One major advantage of earning a two-year degree is that it is much less expensive than paying for a four-year school. Two years is naturally going to cost less than four, and two-year graduates enter the workplace and start earning a paycheck sooner than their four-year counterparts.

The latest statistics from the College Board show that average yearly total tuition and fees at a public two-year college is $2,191, compared to $5,491 at a four-year public college. That cost leaps to more than $21,000 on average for a year at a private four-year school.

With college costs relatively low, some two-year students overlook the idea of applying for financial aid at all. But the fact is, college dollars are available whether you're going to a trade school, community college, or university. About a third of all Pell Grants go to two-year public school students, and while two-year students receive a much smaller percentage of other aid programs, the funding is there for many who apply.

How Does Aid Work?

Financial aid comes in two basic forms: merit-based and need-based.

Merit-based awards are typically funds that recognize a particular talent or quality you may have, and they are given by private organizations, colleges, and the government. Merit-based awards range from scholarships for good writing to prizes for those who have shown promise in engineering. There are thousands of scholarships available for students who shine in academics, music, art, science, and more. Resources on how to get these awards are provided later in this chapter.

Need-based awards are given according to your ability to pay for college. In general, students from families that have less income and fewer assets receive more financial aid. To decide how much of this aid you qualify for, schools look at your family's income, assets, and other information regarding your finances. You provide this information on a financial aid form—usually the federal government's Free Application for Federal Student Aid (FAFSA). Based on the financial details you provide, the school of your choice calculates your Expected Family Contribution (EFC). This is the amount you are expected to pay toward your education each year.

Once your EFC is determined, a school uses this simple formula to figure out your financial aid package:

Cost of attendance at the school

– **Your EFC**

– **Other outside aid (private scholarships)**

= **Need**

Schools put together aid packages that meet that need using loans, work-study, and grants.

Know Your School

When applying to a school, it's a good idea to find out their financial aid policy and history. Read over the school literature or contact the financial aid office and find out the following:

✔ *Is the school accredited?* Schools that are not accredited usually do not offer as much financial aid and are not eligible for federal programs.

✔ *What is the average financial aid package at the school?* The typical award size may influence your decision to apply or not.

✔ *What are all the types of assistance available?* Check if the school offers federal, state, private, or institutional aid.

✔ *What is the school's loan default rate?* The default rate is the percentage of students who took out federal student loans and failed to repay them on time. Schools that have a high default rate are often not allowed to offer certain federal aid programs.

✔ *What are the procedures and deadlines for submitting financial aid?* Policies can differ from school to school.

✔ *What is the school's definition of satisfactory academic progress?* To receive financial aid, you have to maintain your academic performance. A school may specify that you keep up at least a C+ or B average to keep getting funding.

✔ *What is the school's job placement rate?* The job placement rate is the percentage of students who find work in their field of study after graduating.

You'll want a school with a good placement rate so you can earn a good salary that may help you pay back any student loans you have.

Be In It to Win It

The key to getting the most financial aid possible is filling out the forms, and you have nothing to lose by applying. Most schools require that you file the FAFSA, which is *free* to submit, and you can even do it online. For more information on the FAFSA, visit the Web site at http://www.fafsa.ed.gov. If you have any trouble with the form, you can call 1-800-4-FED-AID for help.

To receive aid using the FAFSA, you must submit the form soon after January 1 prior to the start of your school year. A lot of financial aid is delivered on a first-come, first-served basis, so be sure to apply on time.

Filing for aid will require some work to gather your financial information. You'll need details regarding your assets and from your income tax forms, which will include the value of all your bank accounts and investments. The form also asks if you have other siblings in college, the age of your parents, or if you have children. These factors can determine how much aid you receive.

Three to four weeks after you submit the FAFSA, you receive a document called the Student Aid Report (SAR). The SAR lists all the information you provided in the FAFSA and tells you how much you'll be expected to contribute toward school, or your Expected Family Contribution (EFC). It's important to review the information on the SAR carefully and make any corrections right away. If there are errors on this document, it can affect how much financial aid you'll receive.

The Financial Aid Package

Using information on your SAR, the school of your choice calculates your need (as described earlier) and puts together a financial aid package. Aid packages are often built with a combination of loans, grants, and work-study. You may also have won private scholarships that will help reduce your costs.

Keep in mind that aid awarded in the form of loans has to be paid back with interest just like a car loan. If you don't pay back according to agreed upon terms, you can go into *default*. Default usually occurs if you've missed payments for 180 days. Defaulted loans are often sent to collection agencies, which can charge costly fees and even take money owed out of your wages. Even worse, a defaulted loan is a strike on your credit history. If you have a negative credit history, lenders may deny you a mortgage, car loan, or other personal loan. There's also financial incentive for paying back on time—many lenders will give a 1 percent discount or more for students who make consecutive timely payments. The key is not to borrow more than you can afford. Know exactly how much your monthly payments will be on a loan when it comes due and estimate if those monthly payments will fit in your future budget. If you ever do run into trouble with loan payments, don't hesitate to contact your lender and see if you can come up with a new payment arrangement—lenders want to help you pay rather than see you go into default. If you have more than one loan, look into loan consolidation, which can lower overall monthly payments and sometimes lock in interest rates that are relatively low.

The Four Major Sources of Aid

U.S. Government Financial Aid

The federal government is the biggest source of financial aid. To find all about federal aid programs, visit http://www.studentaid.fed.gov or call 1-800-4-FED-AID with any questions. Download the free brochure *Funding Education Beyond High School,* which tells you all the details on federal programs. To get aid from federal programs you must be a regular student working toward a degree or certificate in an eligible program. You also have to have a high school diploma or equivalent, be a U.S. citizen or eligible non-citizen and have a valid Social Security number (check http://www.ssa.gov for info). If you are a male aged 18–25, you have to register for the Selective Service. (Find out more about that requirement at http://www.sss.gov or call 1-847-688-6888.) You must also certify that you are not in default on a student loan and that you will use your federal aid only for educational purposes.

Some specifics concerning federal aid programs can change a little each year, but the major programs are listed here and the fundamentals stay the same from year to year. (Note that amounts you receive generally depend on your enrollment status—whether it be full-time or part-time.)

Pell Grant

For students demonstrating significant need, this award has been ranging between $400 and $4,050. The size of a Pell grant does not depend on how much other aid you receive.

Supplemental Educational Opportunity Grant (SEOG)

Again for students with significant need, this award ranges from $100 to $4,000 a year. The size of the SEOG can be reduced according to how much other aid you receive.

Work-Study

The Federal Work-Study Program provides jobs for students showing financial need. The program encourages community service and work related to a student's course of study. You earn at least minimum wage and are paid at least once a month. Again, funds must be used for educational expenses.

Perkins Loans

With a low interest rate of 5 percent, this program lets students who can document the need borrow up to $4,000 a year.

Stafford Loans

These loans are available to all students regardless of need. However, students with need receive *subsidized* Staffords, which do not accrue interest while you're in school or in deferment. Students without need can take *unsubsidized* Staffords, which do accrue interest while you are in school or in deferment. Interest rates vary but can go no higher than 8.25 percent. Loan amounts vary too, according to what year of study you're in and whether you are financially dependent on your parents or not. Students defined as independent of their parents can borrow much more. (Students who have their own kids are also defined as independent. Check the exact qualifications for independent and dependent status on the federal government Web site http://www.studentaid.fed.gov.)

PLUS Loans

These loans for parents of dependent students are also available regardless of need. Parents with good credit can borrow up to the cost of attendance minus any other aid received. Interest rates are variable but can go no higher than 9 percent.

Tax Credits

Depending on your family income, qualified students can take federal tax deductions for education with maximums ranging from $1,500 to $2,000.

Americorps

This program provides full-time educational awards in return for community service work. You can work before, during, or after your postsecondary education and use the funds either to pay current educational expenses or to repay federal student loans. Americorps participants work assisting teachers in Head Start, helping on conservation projects, building houses for the homeless, and doing other good works. For more information, visit http://www.americorps.gov

State Financial Aid

All states offer financial aid, both merit-based and need-based. Most states use the FAFSA to determine eligibility, but you'll have to contact your state's higher education agency to find out the exact requirements. You can get contact information for your state at http://www.bcol02.ed.gov/Programs/EROD/org_list.cfm. Most of the state aid programs are available only if you study at a school in the state where you reside. Some states are very generous, especially if you're attending a state college or university. California's Cal Grant program gives needy state residents free tuition at in-state public universities.

School-Sponsored Financial Aid

The school you attend may offer its own loans, grants, and work programs. Many have academic- or talent-based scholarships for top-performing students. Some two-year programs offer cooperative education opportunities where you combine classroom study with off-campus work related to your major. The work gives you hands-on experience and some income, ranging from $2,500 to $15,000 per year depending on the program. Communicate with your school's financial aid department and make sure you're applying for the most aid you can possibly get.

Private Scholarships

While scholarships for students heading to four-year schools may be more plentiful, there are awards for the two-year students. Scholarships reward students for all sorts of talent—academic, artistic, athletic, technical, scientific, and more. You have to invest time hunting for the awards that you might qualify for. The Internet now offers many great scholarship search services. Some of the best ones are:

> The College Board (http://www.collegeboard.com/pay)
> FastWeb! (http://www.fastweb.monster.com)
> MACH25 (http://www.collegenet.com)
> Scholarship Research Network (http://www.srnexpress.com)
> SallieMae's College Answer (http://www.collegeanswer.com)

Note: Be careful of scholarship-scam services that charge a fee for finding you awards but end up giving you nothing more than a few leads that you could have gotten for free with a little research on your own. Check out the Federal Trade Commission's Project ScholarScam (http://www.ftc.gov/bcp/conline/edcams/scholarship).

In your hunt for scholarship dollars, be sure to look into local community organizations (the Elks Club, Lions Club, PTA, etc.), local corporations, employers (your employer or your parents' may offer tuition assistance), trade groups, professional associations (National Electrical Contractors Association, etc.), clubs (Boy Scouts, Girl Scouts, Distributive Education Club of America, etc.), heritage organizations (Italian, Japanese,

Chinese, and other groups related to ethnic origin), church groups, and minority assistance programs.

Once you find awards you qualify for, you have to put in the time applying. This usually means filling out an application, writing a personal statement, and gathering recommendations.

General Scholarships

A few general scholarships for students earning two-year degrees are

Coca-Cola Scholars Foundation, Inc.
Coca-Cola offers 350 thousand-dollar scholarships (http://www.coca colascholars.org) per year specifically for students attending two-year institutions.

Phi Theta Kappa (PTK)
This organization is the International Honor Society of the Two-Year College. PTK is one of the sponsors of the All-USA Academic Team program, which annually recognizes 60 outstanding two-year college students (http://scholarships.ptk.org). First, Second, and Third Teams, each consisting of 20 members, are selected. The 20 First Team members receive stipends of $2,500 each. All 60 members of the All-USA Academic Team and their colleges receive extensive national recognition through coverage in *USA TODAY*. There are other great scholarships for two-year students listed on this Web site.

Hispanic Scholarship Fund (HSF)
HSF's High School Scholarship Program (http://www.hsf.net/scholar ship/programs/hs.php) is designed to assist high school students of Hispanic heritage obtain a college degree. It is available to graduating high school seniors who plan to enroll full-time at a community college during the upcoming academic year. Award amounts range from $1,000 to $2,500.

The Military
All branches of the military offer tuition dollars in exchange for military service. You have to decide if military service is for you. The Web site http://www.myfuture.com attempts to answer any questions you might have about military service.

Lower Your Costs

In addition to getting financial aid, you can reduce college expenses by being a money-smart student. Here are some tips.

Use Your Campus

Schools offer perks that some students never take advantage of. Use the gym. Take in a school-supported concert or movie night. Attend meetings and lectures with free refreshments.

Flash Your Student ID

Students often get discounts at movies, museums, restaurants, and stores. Always be sure to ask if there is a lower price for students and carry your student ID with you at all times. You can often save 10 to 20 percent on purchases.

Budget Your Funds

Writing a budget of your income and expenses can help you be a smart spender. Track what you buy on a budget chart. This awareness will save you dollars.

Share Rides

Commuting to school or traveling back to your hometown? Check and post on student bulletin boards for ride shares.

Buy Used Books

Used textbooks can cost half as much as new. Check your campus bookstore for deals and also try http://www.eCampus.com and http://www.bookcentral.com

Put Your Credit Card in the Freezer

That's what one student did to stop overspending. You can lock your card away any way you like, just try living without the ease of credit for awhile. You'll be surprised at the savings.

A Two-Year Student's Financial Aid Package

Minnesota State Colleges and Universities provides this example of how a two-year student pays for college. Note how financial aid reduces his out-of-pocket cost to about $7,000 per year.

Jeremy's Costs for One Year

Jeremy is a freshman at a two-year college in the Minnesota. He has a sister in college, and his parents own a home but have no other significant savings. His family's income: $42,000.

College Costs for One Year

Tuition	$3,437
Fees	$388
Estimated room and board*	$7,200
Estimated living expenses**	$6,116
Total cost of attendance	*$17,141*

Jeremy's Financial Aid

Federal grants (does not require repayment)	$2,800
Minnesota grant (does not require repayment)	$676
Work-study earnings	$4,000
Student loan (requires repayment)	$2,625
Total financial aid	*$10,101*

Total cost to Jeremy's family | *$7,040*

* Estimated cost reflecting apartment rent rate and food costs. The estimates are used to calculate the financial aid. If a student lives at home with his or her parents, the actual cost could be much less, although the financial aid amounts may remain the same.

** This is an estimate of expenses including transportation, books, clothing, and social activities.

Index